Copyright © 2018 by Linda Hunt

All rights reserved. This book or any portion thereof may not be reproduced or used in any manner whatsoever without the express written permission of the publisher except for the use of brief quotations in a book review or scholarly journal.

All scripture references listed herein are taken from
The King James Bible version unless stated otherwise.

First Edition: 2018

ISBN 978-1-5323-7087-8

YAH-Scribe Publishing, LLC
830 Saint Claire, Apt E
Grosse Point, Michigan 48230
www.YAHSCRIBE.com

Beth,
Thank-you for your support & love over the years. May God truly bless & heal you & your family. Nothing is to hard for God!
Love
Linda

Amen Sister!

LINDA HUNT

Dedication

This book is dedicated to my Mother Fannie Gary.

Thank you, Mom, for always believing in me and having the highest desire to see your baby girl achieve her life's goals. You were always so proud of my achievements. It blessed you to see me serving in the house of God and ministering the Word of God. When I graduated with my Bachelor's Degree in Theology, although you were not there to see me walk across the stage, I know you were there in spirit because I felt your presence. I carry your spirit inside of me and as I continue to make strides in life. I will always be eternally grateful for having been the best mother a girl could possibly have.

Love your baby girl,

Linda

Foreword

If there has ever been a time when the countless number of women from every nation, and economic status need hope, motivation and a now Word, this is that time. Amen Sister! is a phenomenal masterpiece written skillfully by Ms. Linda Hunt. This extraordinary book will help navigate the reader through "life's" maze. Linda has done an amazing job in integrating her personal experiences, Biblical truths and familiar stories relative to the topic covered to enable the reader to better understanding the messages being presented.

When I initially heard the title, I envisioned women in the church dancing, clapping their hands and loudly saying "Amen" to the preacher's' sermon. But, as I read chapter upon chapter, {though you will still find many opportunities to shout "amen," over and over again,} it is so much more profound, powerful and transformational than ever.

I have known Linda, {affectionately known as Elder Linda,} for nearly thirty years. I met her while she was serving in ministry and later became a mentor and coach. She is a woman of integrity and sound character who displays copious wisdom in matters of life and particularly that of being a Godly woman, intelligent and faithful.

Linda has a depth that far supersedes the scope of Amen Sister! This book will help guide the hopeless, confused, hurting, as well as, build, encourage and motivate women to birth their dreams, fulfill their purpose and take the limits off. Amen Sister! will provide practical insight, beneficial keys, and instructions for both individuals and groups. This book is a "change agent" and I would suggest its' use in Bible Studies and journaling exercises.

I highly recommend Amen Sister! and appreciate the life and ministry of Linda and her writing such a superb book to heal and inspire women around the world to succeed. Linda comes from an exceptional family and spiritual background with a proven testimony that encourages other women to glorify God in their personal lives and ministries.

Dr. Velma Rosemond Clopton, Apostle
Founder/Realms of Glory Prophetic Ministry
& Discipleship Training
Mesa, AZ

Table of Contents

What Does "Amen" Mean? 15

I Have a Destiny 16

There's a Queen in You 18

Women Without Limits 19

This Is Your Season 21

Most Wonderful Love 23

He Restoreth My Soul 25

Stolen Identity 27

Behold, I Do A New Thing 30

It's Time to Give Birth 33

Time of Transition 35

Surviving the War 37

River of Prosperity 39

The Assignment 42

Tear Down Your Walls 45

Daddy's Home 48

I Who Have Nothing to Give 51

A Promise 53

The Lioness Women 55

The Question Is 58

A Kingdom Breaking Through 60

Discovering Your Roots 63

My Body, His Temple 65

A Kingdom Woman 67
The Wounded Heart 69
The Perfect Storm 74
Minding Your Own Business 76
Your Womb Is Blessed 78
Shifting Lanes 80
The Fragrance of Prayer 83
Waiting On God 85
Reveal Yourself to Me 87
Living On Purpose 89
A Womb or A Tomb 93
God I'm in A Crisis 95
The Power of a Praying Man 97
Marred by Life 99
We Need Sisters 102
How Does Your Garden Grow? 104
The Fruit Bowl Concept 107
You're A Masterpiece 109
Obey the Stop Signs 112
What Is Your Passion? 114
Remove the Clutter 116
The Game Changer 118
Too Much Power 121
My Center 123
I Am My Wealth 125
Don't Desert Your Desert 127

Favoring the King 131

The Story of the Butterfly 133

Blind Spots 134

Roadside Assistance 136

The Necessity to Achieve Your Destiny 139

Hurt but Not Hurting 142

Enhanced Beauty 144

I Am My Own Rescue 146

New Face. Old Building 149

No Longer in Bankruptcy 151

Intercessory Prayers 153

Bringing Closure 155

Endorsements

The word "Amen" is commonly used in a church setting when the preacher is preaching or at the end of a prayer. Although that is true, without a doubt, author Linda Hunt has given profound words of wisdom to her sisters all over the world – both in and outside of the church walls. You will get the feeling that she is sitting and talking to you, person to person.

After editing numerous books over the past three decades, from time-to-time some books come my way that are so rich that I just want to read them – not edit. However, in this case, I have done both with great pleasure. If you or someone you know needs encouragement and godly wisdom, this is the book for you and them. Get two copies. They will thank you for it!

Dr. Mary D. Edwards, Editor

"Amen Sister!" by Linda Hunt is an awe-inspiring and compelling read. It takes you on a journey of speaking truth into the deepest regions of the heart. Personally, I can attest to the challenge of facing deep hurts and you can overcome them through the experiential and the practical application of truth principals in Amen Sister! It unlocks an enlivening understanding of how God designed us to relate, think, choose and feel in an imperfect world as redeemed Christians. God will use these truths to transform the reader into a greater lover of God and better lover of God's people.

Barbra Gentry-Pugh, RN, MA,
CEO of Heart Expressions Ministries International,
Author of "Every Beat of My Heart"

As I read this book, each chapter mapped out the very journey I either have gone through or the one I am currently experiencing. From the Scriptures, in each chapter, my mother is sharing her own personal conversations and thoughts with God. It is as though she was not only speaking for herself but for every woman.

This book spoke our thoughts out loud that we all can identify with as we each go through life's different journeys. My mother's vulnerability allowed us to personally experience her private moments with God that have brought her into wholeness.

Her deliverance, transformation, and walk with God through journalism have allowed me, as her daughter, to see the power of God in her life. Amen Sister! We are not alone. We are a sisterhood of strong women through Christ Jesus.

Thank you and I love you, Mom,

Your one and only child - Toni

Gratitude

My gratitude is to my Pastors, Apostle Kenneth D. and Prophetess Joyce M. Hogan of Living Bread Westgate Church International in Detroit. I honor you. Thank you so very much for your love and support of God's people. Your love for each other spills over onto your concern and care for His sheep. I thank you for your visible standards for the truth and how to live those truths in our everyday lives.

I thank God for Apostle Corletta and Pastor Gilbert Vaughn who taught me how to pray, serve and to love God. It was at Holy Ghost "The Cathedral" Church where my life was dramatically changed and I came to know the Holy Spirit in an intimate way. It was under your wings my gifts and calling was identified. You walked me through the most troublesome times in my life and it was during those times I learned to journal, pray and seek God. It paid off! "Papa" Gilbert always taught us, "Put a difference between clean and unclean. Between holy and unholy." I still live by those truths.

I give honor to all the Apostolic and Prophetic Gifts that have imparted love and blessings over my life. I am a blessed woman. I'm surrounded by a great company of witnesses too many to mention, but you know who you are. I love you.

To my friend, Prophet, Publisher, and co-laborer in the Media Ministry, Prophet Blaine. Thank you for your gift of love and creativity. You opened up a door for me to take my gift and "The Marketplace Connection" broadcast to the world. The best is yet to come!

Introduction

You are a WINNER!

Sisters, in every situation, "let patience possess your souls" (Luke 21:19). Let all of your life experiences mold you into a new creature in Christ and into the beautiful woman of God He intends you to be, by being patient in the molding and shaping process.

I wish that I could be with each one of you as you face life's challenges to encourage you, but I can't. However, I do know someone who can; His name is Jesus. He knows He hears, He cares and He answers. He is the Burden Bearer and the Carrier of heavy loads. He wants to give you rest because He wants the very best life for you. All your hopes and dreams He wants you to fulfill so others can be blessed by your gifts.

Sisters, my hope also is that you become acquainted and enlightened to know the "Helper," the Holy Spirit. He is your Comforter and wisdom that will lead you into all truth. He is a very present help in your time of need. He is waiting and willing to help you.

Amen Sister!

"Wait on the Lord: be of good courage, and he shall strengthen thine heart: wait, I say, on the Lord" (Ps. 27:14)

What Does Amen Mean?

"Amen" means: It is so. So be it. It is an expression of approval. Amen to all the dreams or goals you may have. It is Amen and so be it. The Word of God says, "Delight thyself also in the Lord: and he shall give thee the desires of thine heart" (Ps.37:4).

Amen Sister! is written to motivate, empower and encourage you to your next level. No matter where you are in life, there is another level coming to you. I come into agreement with you that it is so and so be it. Don't stop dreaming; don't stop hoping, keep putting words to those things you desire to do. Just do it!!

You were put here for a purpose and that purpose is to live life abundantly. The abundant life is more than mediocrity. It's more than just over broke. It's more than just enough. Those that live life in the abundance have more than enough for themselves; they also have something to give away.

When you live the abundant life, you are the lender and not the borrower; the head and not the tail; above and not below. This, my sisters, is the abundant life that Jesus was talking about in St. John 10:10, "I am come that they might have life and that they might have it more abundantly."

The abundant life is meant to be lived on earth. The eternal life is going to heaven. The abundant is having resources of information that can help someone else along their journey. The abundant life is the Zoe life or the God-kind of life.

God has blessed me above what I can ask or think. I know what He has done for me. He can and will do it for you. Just keep striving, keep sowing, and keep giving and one day you will see your life take on a new dimension and purpose.

I Have Destiny in Me

Destiny is something which a person or a thing is destined to do or to be: a predetermined course of events, to settle in advance, to designate, assign or dedicate in advance.

I have destiny in me. I'm on a predetermined course for my life. This is a course that only I can travel. It will take me many places and I will meet many people that have been designed and created for my destiny. It is imperative that I meet these people. They have something for me and I have something for them. It is a mutual exchange.

My destiny is God's plan and purpose for my life and those plans will be accomplished. Many times in my life I have questioned God, "What is Your plan for my life?" At some of the lowest points in my life, God has reassured me that He still has a plan and that plan will unfold. I have found myself hurt, lonely, with feelings of rejection and wondering how God could possibly have a plan for my life.

Well, my sister, I assure you that in the midst of my trials, God spoke either to me directly, through a servant of the Lord, or through His word and let me know that He loved me and that His plan is still good and not evil.

God wants you to know that He does have a destiny for you. He has a predetermined, well thought out course for your life and your course is like no one else's. He said even before you were in your mother's womb, God said I knew you. While you were just a beam in your mother and father's eye God already determined the path you would take.

You are not a mistake. He has so much work for you to do. He chooses not to do it alone or without you. All he really wants is to bless you and to use you for His Glory. You are a representation of His glory.

Your greatest hour, your greatest season awaits you, my sister. Dust off those plans and those goals, roll up your sleeves and let's go to work. You were created for this. Yes, the road gets rough and the hill gets hard to climb, but we were made for the push! Push until something happens.

Amen Sister!

"For I know the thoughts that I think toward you, saith the Lord, thoughts of peace, and not of evil, to give you an expected end" (Jeremiah 29:11)

There's A Queen in You

There is a queen in you waiting to be developed, wanting to be fulfilled. She longs to break out of you, but you will not let her. She's greater than that woman you have come to know, love and be comfortable with. She longs to take you to the higher level of who you are and use all of those gifts and talents that you have hidden for so long. She wants to use your wisdom and all of your life's experiences to bless and enrich others.

A queen is someone that will take the responsibility for leadership and dominate in whatever she sets out to accomplish. She is someone that mentors and reproduces others to reach their goals, while she is striving to meet her own. She cannot be jealous and envious of others that are different from her, but she celebrates, collaborates and applauds those differences.

A queen is the next most important person to the king. Therefore, for those of you that want to be married, there is a king somewhere just waiting for you. He is waiting to take you to your rightful place of rulership. He's waiting for you to come and sit next to him on his throne. Do not settle for a prince; you are a queen; go for the King and all that He has prepared for you and His Kingdom.

Jesus is King of Kings and He has a place prepared for you, His queen, to come and rule with Him forever. Prepare yourself now. Get to know this King so when He comes again you will be prepared to rule and reign with Him forever.

My sisters, look like royalty, seek after royalty, carry yourself like the royalty you are and become that royalty because your "Royal King" is waiting for you. There is a queen in you.

> "And if I go and prepare a place for you, I will come again, and receive you unto myself; that where I am, there ye may be also" (John 14:3)

Women Without Limits

You are a woman called to do great things. You're a woman that has no limit to what you can and will achieve.

As I reflect on the responsibility and the awesome privilege of writing this book, I realize that I am a woman without limits. I never dreamed that I would one day write a book. I've always liked to write out my thoughts in the form of journaling during the difficult times in my life. My writing, during those difficult times, has been a way of bringing perspective to my problem-solving. It was my way of talking to God. He has answered many of my prayers and there are others still to be answered.

We have a God who is limitless. There is no limit to what He can do in a life yielded unto Him. The limitations we have are the limits we place on ourselves. His desire is that each one would soar like an eagle and go to the highest heights in this life.

Soar, soar, soar my sisters. Take the limits off God. Take the limits off yourself and achieve those dreams you have put to the side. There should be no limits or boundaries to what you want to see happen in your life. There are no glass ceilings and, if there are, let's begin to break them.

Enlarge your borders, expand your territory, stretch forth your tents and strengthen your stakes. Go back and dust off those broken dreams. Put some hope in those dreams and begin to walk by faith and see them come to pass. They're not too old; they're not too big, and they're not too ridiculous. You can do all those things that you desire to do. Just do it!

Don't let procrastination rob you another day of fulfilling those things that you have so longed to do. Don't let excuses say to you that you can't do it. You can do it! Just do it!

If it means living right, I can do it. If it's talking right, I can do it. If it means loving right, I can do it. If it's thinking right, I can do it. Say with me: "With God, I can do all things. I am a woman without limits!"

Amen Sister!

"I can do all things through Christ which strengtheneth me" (Philippians 4:13).

This Is Your Season

It's your season to begin to become all that you can be naturally and spiritually. This is a time that you can begin to see your prayers answered and dreams come true. You don't need to wait any longer; your season is here. There is a time for planting and then there is a time for reaping. If you have sown any seeds, you must know that you can look for a harvest. This is a principle that really works.

What are you sowing? Are you sowing seeds of love, peace, and joy? You can begin to look for the seeds to come back to you in a very special way. The Bible tells us to, "Cast thy bread upon the waters: for after many days you will find it again" (Eccl. 11:1). God is blessing His people; those that will stand faithful to the end. The race is not given to the swift or the strong, but he that endures to the end. If you endure, you will reap your harvest. This is your season, Sister.

Keep planting, keep on loving, and keep encouraging. God has not forgotten your labor of love. Do you have seed in the ground? This is your season of grace and favor. The favor of God is better than money. He will reward you. This is your time for God to begin to shift things in your favor. What has been against you will now be for you. If God is for you, who can be against you?

I stand in agreement with you that your harvest time has come. It's not just your time. It's your turn.

Amen Sister!

"As long as the earth endures, seedtime and harvest, cold and heat, summer and winter, day and night will never cease" (Genesis 8:22)

Journal Notes

*"**Lord, thou hast been our dwelling place in all generations**"*
(Ps. 90:1)

Most Wonderful Love

Everyone longs to give themselves completely to someone; to have a deep soul relationship with another, to be loved thoroughly and exclusively.

God says…

"No, not until you are satisfied and fulfilled and content with being loved by Me alone, with giving yourself totally, unreservedly to Me alone. I love you, My child, and until you discover that only in Me is your satisfaction to be found, you will not be capable of the perfect human relationship that I have planned for you.

"You will never be united with another until you are united with Me…exclusively of anyone or any other desires and longings. I want you to stop planning, stop wishing and allow Me to give you the most thrilling plan that you cannot even imagine. I want you to have the very best.

"Please allow Me to bring it to you. Just keep your eyes on Me, expecting the greatest things…Keep experiencing the satisfaction of knowing that I AM. Keep learning and listening to the things I tell you. You must be patient and wait.

"Do not be anxious and do not worry. Do not look around at the things others have gotten or what I gave them. Do not look at the things you think you want. Just keep looking at Me or you will miss what I want to give to you. And then, when you are ready, and the one I have for you is ready, know that I am working even this minute to have both of you ready at the same time. Until you are both satisfied exclusively with Me and the life I have prepared for you, you will not be able to experience the love that exemplifies your relationship with Me and this perfect love.

"And Dear One, I want you to have this wonderful love. I want you to see in the flesh a picture of your relationship with Me and to enjoy materially and concretely the everlasting union of beauty and perfection. I AM God."

~Author Unknown.~

no copyright infringement intended

Amen Sister!

Behold, what manner of love the Father hath bestowed upon us, that we should be called the sons of God: therefore the world knoweth us not, because it knew him not" (I John 3:1)

God so loved the world, that he gave His only begotten Son, that whosoever believeth in Him would not perish but have everlasting life. (John 3:16)

Nor height, nor depth, nor any other creature, shall be able to separate us from the **love of God**, which is in Christ Jesus our Lord. (Romans 8:39)

He Restoreth My Soul

Jesus is the Restorer of the soul. He wants to restore your peace of mind, joy, finances, marriage and loved ones. He wants to touch you and make you whole. He wants you to become whole in your body, soul, and mind. Once you become whole, you are no longer fractured and divided on the inside. Jesus said in John 17:22, "And the glory which thou gavest me I have given them; that they may be one, even as we are one."

Jesus desires that we come into oneness, wholeness with ourselves, as well as with others. He wants to completely rid us of all our present and past wounds. Before we can be joined to another, we have to be whole and one with ourselves.

If we are fractured and divided on the inside of our bodies, we are not in harmony with our spirit. The body becomes disconnected and begins to divide against itself. Our hair begins to break off, split ends appear and stress takes place. Our skin begins to break out, and our stomach begins to produce acid causing ulcers.

The whole body begins to become discontented with who we are and how God has made us. Gloom and depression begin to set in, along with suicidal thoughts and nothing seems to satisfy. But there is hope. David said, "Yea, though I walk through the valley of the shadow of death, I will fear no evil: for thou art with me; thy rod and thy staff they comfort me" (Psa. 23:4).

God's rod and staff will comfort you in your midnight hour. He will take you through every valley and every dry place in your life then bring you to higher ground. He is with you in the midst of your troubles and in the midst of your sorrows. All your tears He wants to wipe away so you can be healed and be whole again.

When you are whole you can see things through the eyes of faith. You believe that you are capable of doing great things. You believe the impossible. You will begin to smile again. You will begin to love again. You will begin to hope again. That His ultimate desire for each of us to live the abundant life. He came that we might have this life and have it more abundantly, in our lifetime.

Let Him be the Restorer of everything that is breached and broken in your life. He is the Repairer of the breach. The Restorer of the paths you dwell in. He can and will mend you and bind you together for His glory. To God be the glory.

Amen Sister!

"The Lord is my shepherd. I shall not be in want. He makes lie down in green pastures; He leads me beside quiet waters; He restores my soul"
(Ps. 23:1-3)

Stolen Identity

In the days and times we are living in, there is a great deal of concern regarding stolen identity. It is such a crisis that the government and corporations have to protect the innocent by policies and procedures of the Federal Trade Commission and the Privacy Act Statement.

You can no longer feel safe giving information such as your social security number, bank account or credit card information over the phone or the Internet. You don't know who is on the other end of the phone or, more importantly, who is standing in front of you looking you right in the eye that might use your personal information to defraud you. Who would have thought 20 years ago that we would be in such an increased present-day dilemma?

However, the worst kind of stolen identity is allowing someone to steal your God-given identity. God asked Adam in the garden, "Who told you that you were naked?" (Gen 3:11a).

After disobeying God's order, Adam lost the original plan and purpose for his life and that was to be innocent of any and all evil. Suddenly, knowing he was naked, he hid.

The woman admitted she had been deceived, and she too had disobeyed God's orders. The Bible says," And when the woman saw that the tree was good for food and that it was pleasant to the eyes, and a tree to be desired to make one wise, she took of the fruit thereof, and did eat, and gave also unto her husband with her; and he did eat" (Gen. 3:6).

Have you, at some point and time in your life, allowed the enemy to talk to your mind and self-esteem and you say, "I can't be this. I can't do this. I can't make these changes in my life, in my home, in my marriage, in my relationships, on my job. I can't do that?" Who told you that? Yes, you can!

You can be that man, woman boy or girl that God in His original plan and purpose intended you to be. You can get that degree, you can buy that new car, and you can buy that house. You can move to another city and start a new life for yourself. You can start that business. You can be all that you want to be. Just do it.

If you are in a life-threatening relationship, seek help or get out. If you are doing drugs, smoking cigarettes and you want help, you can get help and quit. Don't be deceived. Who told you that you couldn't do it? Who told you that?

Stealing your credit card or bank information is one thing, but to let someone steal your God-given liberty is far more damaging. What God planned for each of us is to give us a hope and a future and to bring us to our expected end. There is an expectation that He already has planned for you. Don't be deceived! You can reach your goals and be all that you want to be. You can start right now. Today is the day of your deliverance.

Yes, you can, you will, and you must do it. Who said that it would be easy? Who told you that? But you can do it. Who told you that you were too old, too fat, too skinny, too young, not the right height, not the right gender, came from the wrong family, lived on the wrong side of the tracks, don't have enough money? Who told you that?

The only reason the enemy wants to stop you because he's had a glimpse of your future and knows that you are a threat to the kingdom of darkness. He wants to steal your God-given purpose so that you can't help others become liberated and free. But, to become free you must because there are others that need what you have. Don't ever minimize what you have. It is to be a blessing to someone else.

From this day forward, don't let another moment of your God-given identity be stolen from you. Make up your mind. Tell yourself, "I can be all that He destined me to be." Who told you that you couldn't? Who told you that? Arise! Receive it. Believe it. Achieve it!

Amen Sister!

"The thief comes only to steal and kill and destroy; I have come that they may have life, and have it to the full."
(John 10:10)

Behold. I Do a New Thing

Behold, all things become new and all the old things are passing away in your lives, my sisters. "Behold" means to look, listen or to take notice of what is being done in your life. You can choose to look at the positive or the negative in life. Life is just life and in every life, some rain must fall. There is no getting around the issues of life. Keep on living and you will experience the many phases of life: the ups and the downs, the highs and the lows, the happy and the sad. It takes all of these experiences to make us the women that we presently are.

God has proven himself to me over and over again. He has shown me that all the experiences in my life were necessary. The experiences might not have felt so good, but they were all working together for my good. It took all of that to make and shape me into the woman that I am. The experience did not come to destroy me. It came to make me strong.

I had to learn to get outside of myself and my feelings to see the bigger picture. Sometimes you have to get outside the picture frame of life to appreciate the real beauty of the picture that God is trying to create for your life. Your life is like a canvas and every day God is drawing on and painting on your canvas. He is creating a beautiful, masterful picture just for you.

I could not be the woman that I am today without the experience. The experience became my teacher in order that I might help someone else if I wouldn't allow myself to become selfish. I truly see my life as a blessing to others around me.

My sisters, God is doing a new thing. This is the time to see an increase; the year for you to stretch yourself out of the old pattern of thinking and to come into new thoughts. You need to come from among old friends and habits that are holding on to you and weighing you down.

Begin to look for and expect to see new things with new experiences. Ask Him now to change your mindset that you are ready and able to receive the new thing He wants to give you. You can't put new and fresh wine in an old wineskin it becomes damaged.

New things are coming your way, my sisters. New things I do declare! Just wait for them and it will be well worth the wait!

Amen Sister!

"Behold, the former things are come to pass, and new things do I declare: before they spring forth I tell you of them"
(Isaiah 42:9)

Journal Notes

"To every thing there is a season, and a time to every purpose under the heaven" (Ecclesiastes 3:1)

It's Time to Give Birth

God has given women the most miraculous assignment in the world and that is to conceive birth and bring forth life. The Bible says that woman was taken out of the man, but man must be born of a woman. We are man or mankind with the womb and we are known as WO-MAN. What a privilege and honor it is to be able to bring forth all of God's human creation through our wombs. We are distinctively and necessarily different. No one in all the earth can do what we are called to do. We are blessed by the Almighty God.

We also have the same ability to birth the plans and the purposes of God in our lives. This is the real reason we were created. God does have the perfect plan for your life. It is up to you to seek the Lord as to what you were created for and to live a purpose-driven life.

You were put here to be a blessing to someone else. You do have something to contribute. You are a woman of value. Value is not in how many fine clothes you have or what kind of car you drive. Value is how many people are blessed by your life and what you do for those less fortunate than you. Do you love your family? Are you kind and forgiving of others, no matter what they have done? Are you able to bless and not curse, when you know that you have tried to help someone who has stabbed you in the back?

Love is patient, love is kind, and love keeps no record of wrong. To birth the plans and the purposes of God, you must prepare the womb of your heart. The womb of your heart is that place where your choices and decisions are made. It must now go under the examining eyes of God. Is your heart right in the sight of God?

When you examine yourself, are you true to thyself? If you are, you will begin to see the real purpose for which you were created and you can begin to birth that purpose in the earth. It has been said by the late Dr. Myles Munroe that "The richest place in the world is the cemetery." Why? So many people die without birthing the plans and purposes of God in their lives. Don't be one of those people. Birth and keep on birthing what God has for you. Bring your "baby" into the earth realm that you may be a blessing to someone's life and, in the process, you will be blessed.

Your gift is not just for you my Sisters. It is for others that they may be blessed and encouraged by what God is doing in your life. You are someone's template, someone's example. The Scriptures are loaded with examples of real people for you and me to pattern our lives after. And as you read about their lives let it transform you to become someone's pattern. You are blessed to be a blessing.

It's time to birth!

Amen Sister!

"And God blessed them, and God said unto them, Be fruitful, and multiply, and replenish the earth, and subdue it" (Genesis 1:2)

Time of Transition

The world, as we know it today, is in a time and state of transition. There are wars and rumors of wars in the headlines every day. The economic and political arenas are in a frightening state of turmoil. People are concerned about whether they will have jobs and finances to meet their daily needs. They are losing jobs to downsizing and company closings at alarming rates with no idea what tomorrow will bring. These are truly times and seasons of transition.

The transition can also be a time of growth. It can be a time to make changes in your life, your career and your relationships.
It, too, can be a little frightening, because it is a time when nothing seems to be stable; everything in your life and your world seems to be moving.

It's a time when things are being reshaped and reformed. The old and the new seem to be clashing. Things that used to work seems not to work any longer. Things that gave you peace now seem to irritate you. Some people that you thought would always be a part of your life now are drifting away.

There's a paradigm shift going on. The old patterns that used to work no longer work. What used to fit, no longer fits. The plans that you made last year don't seem to be the things you want to do this year. Things just don't seem to be the same. It's nothing wrong. It's just a season of transition.

Take this time to do some inventory. See what might be hindering you from moving in this season of transition. What is weighing me down? Learn to lay aside those things that keep you from moving forward. The transition has come to move you. It has come to move you from something to something.

It has come to move you from one place to another place. It is meant to be positive and not negative. If the situation is not positive while passing through, allow it to run its course. You will emerge stronger on the other side and more equipped to handle your next challenge.

Challenges come and challenges go. Trouble does not last always. You have to move with the cloud and the wind of change to your next destination. Don't get stuck.

Let the challenges propel you to your next dimension, your next level of growth. Life is a series of challenges and transitions, but life is good!

Amen Sister!

"To every thing there is a season, and a time to every purpose under the heaven:" (Ecclesiastes 3:1)

Surviving The War

There are wars and rumors of wars going on all over the world today. There is also a war going on in the lives of God's people. There is a financial war, a spiritual war, social war, emotional war, there's war in our marriages, war to keep our jobs and our homes. War! There is a war on every front, at home and abroad. Terrorism is not limited to a group of people. Terrorism is the frightening day-to-day survival of life.

Stress is high, emotions are high and life seems to be so unsteady now. You can't be certain from one day to the next if that friendly neighbor next door today can be our worst enemy tomorrow. Why? We don't have that same commonality we once called community. When there was a sense of a community, we would make sure the enemy and danger stayed out of our neighborhoods. We would make sure that the drugs stayed away and our children could safely play on our streets or at the local playground. Women were respected, men honored and the elderly were esteemed and cared for. We are in a war for our very survival.

But, having said all of this, the real question is, are you a survivor? Can you say that when the dust settles and clears, "I will still be standing?" I heard a songwriter say, "After you've done all you can, you just stand." You have a part to play in your survival and that is to just stand knowing everything is going to be alright.

He will never leave you or forsake you (Heb. 13:5b). You have to take a stand for that which is right when everything seems to be going wrong. You just have to stand still to see the faithfulness and the deliverance of the Lord.

Yes, sometimes the road gets rocky, times get tight and sometimes we might not know the next series of events, but some way, somehow, things get back on track for us. We must take a stand and just stand. Stand against doubt. Stand against fear. Stand against unbelief. Stand against economic ruin. Stand against sickness. Stand against debt or whatever you must face. Just stand! And when you have stood continue to stand. Daylight is coming. Sunlight is coming. Hope is coming. Success is coming. Wealth is coming. The mate is coming. The house is coming. The car is coming. The job is coming. Just continue to stand!

You might lose some battles; you might lose some things and some people but, remember, by God's grace you will survive the war. Only the strong survive. Are you a survivor? Will you be standing when all is said and done and when the war is over in your life? Will you be a casualty or a survivor? Arise to survive!

Amen Sister!

"Arise [from spiritual depression to a new life], shine [be radiant with the glory and brilliance of the Lord]; for your light has come, And the glory and brilliance of the Lord has risen upon you"
(Isa. 60:1Amp)

River of Prosperity

Around the year 2003, the Lord spoke to me as I sat at my desk. He said to me, "I never desired for my people to depend on one stream of income. I have many streams of income I want to provide for my people. When one stream dries up, I want to continue to be able to provide for them." He gave me a vision of a river with many streams flowing into the river. He called it, "The River of Prosperity."

He told me, "I showed you The River of Prosperity not for information but for a revelation and you will teach My people." He took me to my Bible which I always kept in a drawer close by and directed me to I Kings 17:7. I believe that God was preparing me for what was soon to come, as we saw the economic downturn beginning in the year 2008. So, as He had shown me, one day in the year of 2009, my brook dried up.

I worked in the highly competitive male-dominated car sales industry for over 15 years. The hours were long and fast-paced, as my dealership was one of the top Chrysler dealerships in the Detroit metro area. But everyone in the automotive industry began to feel the economic crunch. Plants began to downsize, dealerships began to close up, sales and earnings began to plummet. We all were just trying to hold on to our individual investments and to our personal properties. But the brook was drying up and drying up fast.

God has given each of us the ability to reach our potential in this life. He has given us many talents and gifts to use and to prosper us. There are many streams that flow into our lives that can bring us wealth and well-being. We use so little of the tools God has placed in us or around us to take our lives to a place of abundance.

Sometimes God allows certain situations in our lives to completely dry up so we will be forced to move to another stream and begin to fish there for new things, ideas or even for new people to come into our lives. We can limit the Hand of God from moving in our lives because of small thinking. We think too small!

God is a good God and He is good all the time. There are many streams of creativity He wants to use in our lives to bring Him glory. I want to encourage you that if the brook has dried up in one area of your life, believe that God has another stream that He wants to open up. He doesn't want us to depend on just one stream to care for us and provide for us. He has many ways that He wants to provide the things we have need of.

He has told us that our thoughts are not His thoughts and our ways are not His ways. (Isaiah 55:8-9). Be open to the Voice of God and ask Him, "What would you have me to do? Open my eyes that I can see the many ways and the many streams You want to use to provide for me. You are the Great Provider, surely You will provide for me."

Amen Sister!

"And the ravens brought him bread and flesh in the morning, and bread and flesh in the evening; and he drank of the brook. And it came to pass after a while, that the brook dried up, because there had been no rain in the land"
(I King 17:6-7)

Journal Notes

"Save now, I beseech thee, O LORD: O LORD, I beseech thee, send now prosperity" (Ps. 118:25).

The Assignment

Assignment: Anything assigned, as a lesson or task. The transfer of a claim, right or property.

Assignor: One who assigns or makes an assignment of any property, right, or interest.

Assignee: A person to whom property, rights, or powers are transferred by another, an agent or trustee.

The most traumatic experience that one could face is dealing with the fact your loved one is dying, or that you may never see them again. However, this was the most precious time for me. It was so full of the purpose and timing of God that my sisters and I shall never, ever forget.

My mother, as she lies on her deathbed, asked me to give her a Word from the Lord. I said to her that the Lord had placed this song in my heart, "If It Had Not Been for the Lord On My Side."

As I sang this song to my mother, I realized that through the hills, valleys, tests, and storms, God had been on her side. I believe at that moment in her journey she needed to be reassured that God was on her side. The Bible says, "For this God is our God for ever and ever: he will be our guide even unto death" (Ps. 48:14).

Mama was making her peace with God and she was getting ready to go. I know that it was hard for her to leave us, but she just needed encouragement that He would be there to guide her through the portals of death and that He would be there to meet her on the other side.

The Lord spoke one word to me as my sisters and I prepared for her funeral, "Assignment." My mother had been given an assignment. My mother had done many wonderful things socially and politically. She was a charter member of a civic group, founder of a woman's political group, a supporter, and member of the NAACP. She even had decided to return to college in her mid-60 years. All of these were good, but this was not her assignment. Everything God created has a purpose and has been assigned to do something. There is nothing in all creation without an assignment. Say to yourself, "I have an assignment."

My mother's assignment was to bring four little girls to the earth, to nurture them, love them, and provide a loving stable home, with Christian values and morals. She was to give them a strong, family-oriented home with a loving father, and she did all of these things. Anyone who knew my mother knew she loved her children. These four little girls would grow up and become women, wives, and mothers, but, more importantly, we would one day find Jesus Christ and do some things she would never do. Her four little girls would do things that would impact the Kingdom of God.

My mother was so proud of her daughters and the work that we were doing for the Lord. Many times my mother would brag to her friends, "This one does this and this one does that; this one is the preacher; this one is the teacher, and this one is in everything at church."

Although my mother was a faithful servant of the church she attended, she never found herself in the ministry. She admired us so very much for our service to God. It made her so proud. She would utilize our gifts to minister to her in many ways. It was the Word of God that strengthened her when she was in the valley of the shadow of death.

She knew that her assignment was about to end here on earth and her new assignment in heaven was about to begin. Mama took the time to inquire one last time and ask each one, "How's your family?" She would wait for the answer and then she'd ask the next one, "How's your family?" She was satisfied everyone was okay.

I was given the assignment to pray for my mother and to help usher her into the presence of the Lord. I understood that God had brought us all together one last time so we could encourage her and that all was well with us and our families.

By my mother's request, I leaned over her bed to hug her and pray. I whispered in her ear, "It is okay, Momma, you can go on. We are going to be okay." I felt her give a sigh of relief. She then prayed for our families that God would take care of us, and we all would be okay. Two days later the Lord came to take her home to be with Him. That was the completion of her assignment here on earth. She passed the test and now she is in the presence of the Lord. Glory to God!

I have one question for you. What is your assignment?
What has God assigned to you to do? Are you working on your assignment? I want to encourage you today to begin to seek the Lord and begin to work on your assignment. One day, the Assignor is coming back to ask the Assignee this question, "Have you finished your assignment?" You are going to have to take the test.

My prayer is you will pass the test; your assignment will be completed; and that you will hear Him say "Well done."

> "Well done, thou good and faithful servant: thou hast been faithful over a few things, I will make thee ruler over many things: enter thou into the joy of thy Lord" (Matt. 25:21)

Amen Sister!

Tear Down your Walls

While at home one day and looking for a good movie to watch, I happened upon the television mini-series, "The Women of Brewster Place." It was on the cable network and starring Oprah Winfrey, Robin Givens and a host of other stars. The movie portrayed a group of strong-willed and determined women who were a portrait of strength and courage. They fought crime, poverty, disenfranchisement, lesbianism, broken relationships, death, gossip, fear and distrust.

They lived in an old dilapidated apartment building with little or no help from the owners. Thus, they decided to organize a tenant association and began to use their united voices to bring change; but fighting their way out of this depressive and oppressive situation was not that easy. There were so much gossip and bitterness between them that it would not allow them to unite and fight the real problem and not each other. They seemed to be caught in a maze of disappointments, troubles, and woes that would not allow them to get out.

Adding to and making their life and matters worse was a sign on a wall at the end of their street: "Dead End." That sign seemed to capsulize their plight. This wall, by city ordinance, blocked the residents off from the rest of the city and became a collection place for refuse and garbage. The wall was just another sign showing how cut off they were from living a productive, prosperous, open and full life. It was a wall of hopelessness and despair. No way out. A dead-end street and a "dead-end life."

One of the high points of this movie came at the end when the character Ceil, portrayed by Lynn Whitfield, returned back to Brewster Place after the tragic loss of her child. This happened while she pleaded with her hopeless and discouraged husband not to leave her after losing his job. Sadly, the child electrocuted herself by sticking a pair of scissors in an electric socket. Ceil went into deep depression and had a mental breakdown, but with the help of Mattie, portrayed by Oprah Winfrey, she managed to gain enough strength to escape her own imprisonment and move to New York City.

But, the epic moment came while all of the community were enjoying a fundraiser to help fix up their building, tragedy strikes again. One of the members gets raped and another mistakenly beaten to death. The character Mattie, so disgusted, said to Etta Mae, (portrayed by Jackee Harry) "That's why I don't trust trying no mo'. The harder folks try, the mo' something comes along and smacks 'em down. It's always something standing in the way of good. Just like that wall blocking this street off and I'm tired of it! 'Yaw hear me? I'm tired of it!"

So Mattie walks slowly to the wall, with a tire iron she picks out of the refuse and she begins to tear down the "Dead End" sign on the wall. Others joined in with her and, with their bare hands, they all begin to tear the wall down, brick by brick. For the first time, they have a sense of freedom and could begin to see the world is bigger than the hopelessness of Brewster Place.

There may be some walls in your life that you have a need to tear down; something that you may feel that is blocking you from your future and your destiny. Maybe you're in a dead-end job, a dead-end relationship, a dead-end career, dead-end weight gain, with no way out. You must have the same determination that Mattie had and free yourself from whatever is imprisoning you, one day at a time, one brick at a time.

You have the power to tear your own walls down. God has given you the power to do all that He has called you to do and be in this life. You, like Mattie, must change your mindset and say, "I'm tired and I'm not going to complain anymore. I'm going to do something about this. Enough is enough."

That same power that raised Jesus from the dead is in you. You have the power to make a change. You have the power to take control of your life and your future. It's time to take your freedom back! It's never too late. Age doesn't matter, money doesn't matter, and material things don't matter. What matters is you getting your life back.

Live your life expansively, out in the open and unapologetically. Get your sexy back. Began to dream again and go after what is rightfully yours. Come out of your hiding place. Stop hiding in the shadows. What has caused you to stop dreaming, hoping and believing? The Word says to you, "Why art thou cast down, O my soul? and why art thou disquieted in me? Hope thou in God" (Ps. 42:5a). Put your faith back to work by putting your hope again in God!

Tear down those walls and don't stop until every brick is gone and you can see your way out to freedom. Don't just break through, break out!

Amen Sister!

"See, I have engraved you on the palms of my hands; your walls are ever before me"
(Isaiah 49:16)

Daddy's Home

I grew up in a small town on the outskirts of Pittsburgh, Pennsylvania, in a housing development known as the Whitaker Projects, which was a place of community and love. The Whitaker Projects, built during the Second World War, was meant to be housing for soldiers returning from the war, but instead became affordable housing for families.

Even though our families didn't have much money, we had a lot of love and concern for one another and for the children in that small town project. There was family unity, and very seldom did you see a one-parent home. The fathers were present in the homes, taking care of the wife and children and holding steady jobs; they were the protectors of the neighborhood. All the families looked after each other and when one person was in need the community pitched in.

Pittsburgh is known for its steel mills, coal mines, mountains, and bridges. Most of the men in the Whitaker Projects worked in the steel mills. Like any other industry, it had its share of layoffs and when the men got laid off the community would unite and have what was called "rent parties," to raise money so they could provide for their families.

The rent parties would consist of the host apartment selling chicken or fish sandwiches, pop, liquor, a friendly game of poker or bid whist card playing. This was the community life of hard-working people trying as best they knew how to raise their families.

As the youngest child in my family of four siblings, I was particularly spoiled by my older siblings and my father. My mother was the disciplinarian, so she made sure we were disciplined in the midst of my father spoiling us.

I remember I always wanted to follow my father around wherever he went and he would say to me, "Daddy will be back home." Whenever I thought Daddy was somewhere in the projects I would search door to door and would say, "Is my daddy here?" He would get so much joy out of me looking for him. Every time he heard my knock, he knew that was his baby knocking for him. My father truly loved his wife and children.

Just as a natural father, you have a heavenly Father who is called, "Abba Father" or "Daddy," and He is always at home waiting for you. He promised to never leave you or forsake you. He is your Provider, your Comforter, your Keeper and your Healer. I praise God for my natural daddy, but my heavenly Daddy is so much more. My natural daddy was with me for a little over 80 years and I thank God for that, but I talked to my heavenly Daddy this morning and He is still at home waiting for my call. I'm still asking, "Is my Daddy home?" I got an answer this morning. And YES He's still at home.

What are you in need of? What is it that you want? Have you talked to Him and told Him about your situation or have you leaned to the arm of flesh for your answers? He loves you so much and He wants the very best for your life and the things that He has not allowed to happen have been for your own protection. His delays are not His denials. Maybe it's just not time yet. Maybe that man is not the one. And maybe, just maybe, God has something so much better for you. Just wait and see.

I know the wait can be painful. I know it seems like a slow process, but He's never late and He's never too early. He's always right on time. Daddy said, "If ye then, being evil, know how to give good gifts unto your children, how much more shall your Father which is in heaven give good things to them that ask him?" (Matt. 7:11).

Think about that. You love your children and He loves His children. He's your Creator. He made you and, more importantly, He loves you unconditionally.

Daddy has given gifts to you without your asking. Are you using those gifts? The best gift Daddy gave you was His love. You are accepted in the Beloved (Eph. 1:6). Know that your Daddy loves you. He wants you to always know that no matter what the situation is He is always at home. If you seek Him, you will find him. If you seek him with all your heart (Deut. 4:29).

Amen Sister!

"And because ye are sons, God hath sent forth the Spirit of his Son into your hearts, crying, Abba, Father" (Gal. 4:6)

This is dedicated to my loving father James A. Gary who was a daddy always available and always at home.

~Deceased April 18, 1987

I Have Nothing to Give

I who have nothing to give except the gift of love.
A love that only a friend could give.
A love that will always live.
A love that will lend a helping hand.
A love that will listen whenever you need a friend.
A love that will help you fight when you are right.
A love that will not pass judgment, but gently suggest when you're wrong.
A love that will last all year long.
I said that I had nothing to give, but I didn't see.
What I have to give to you is really me.

By Linda Hunt to my friend Marie Annette Hill-Jackson
Love is the gift that keeps on giving.

Amen Sister!

"I have shewed you all things, how that so labouring ye ought to support the weak, and to remember the words of the Lord Jesus, how he said, It is more blessed to give than to receive"
(Acts 20:35)

Journal Notes

"For no matter how many promises God has made, 'Yes' in Christ. And so through Him, 'Amen' is spoken by us to the glory of God"
(2 Corinthians 1:20).

A Promise

What exactly is a promise? A promise is a pledge to do or not to do something; assurance one will do a particular thing; that a particular thing will happen.

As I reflected on the word promise, I thought about my mother's oldest sister, the matriarch of our family. My aunt Arkansas Jackson asked God to allow her to live to be 100 years old. She believed by faith that she would live to see 100 years. God gave her favor and she lived to see 100 ½ years. She lived a healthy and full life, free of diseases in her body, just old age had taken over.

The Bible says in Genesis 21:1-2 NIV, "Now the LORD was gracious to Sarah as he had said, and the LORD did for Sarah what he had promised. ² Sarah became pregnant and bore a son to Abraham in his old age, at the very time God had promised him."

Sarah was close to 76 years old and Abraham was nearing 86 years old when Sarah grew impatient and told Abraham to sleep with her slave girl named Hagar, she would have a child and her son would become their "**promised son.**"

Well, it happened, Hagar got pregnant and bore Abraham a son and they called him Ishmael. Sarah became jealous and she put Hagar and her son out. God had appeared to Abraham by angels several times and promised him a son that would come from his own body, but as Abraham and Sarah grew older it looked like it might not happen. Sarah even laughed when the angel told her, "I will surely return to you about this time next year, and Sarah your wife will have a son" (Gen 18:10NIV)

"Now the LORD was gracious to Sarah as he had said, and the LORD did for Sarah what he had promised. Sarah became pregnant and bore a son to Abraham in his old age, at the very time God had promised him." (Gen 21:1)

How many times have you gotten impatient and tried to help God out with the promises He has made to you, and even gone ahead of Him to make them happen? There are over 5,000 promises in the Bible and all the promises of God are yea and amen or, so be it. If He has spoken a promise to you, it will happen.

Some of us are living with our mistakes by not waiting on God and having to live with the very "Ishmaels" of our lives. The mistakes we made by choosing the wrong mates, wrong friends, the wrong house, the wrong car, the wrong career, the Ishmaels of life.

But, be of good cheer. Just as Abraham and Sarah, God has not forgotten you. Abraham believed God. The promise was yet to come and God gave him favor. The promise wasn't based on what he did. It was based on what God said because a promise is a promise.

Amen Sister!

"God is not human, that he should lie, not a human being, that he should change his mind. Does he speak and then not act? Does he promise and not fulfill? I have received a command to bless; he has blessed, and I cannot change it" (Numbers 23:19-20)

A Lioness Woman

      The lioness animals are amazing creatures to watch. I am not an expert on lions or lionesses, but I have developed into a fascinated observer. There are so many similarities between the lioness and women and how they relate to their cubs, another female lioness, and the male lion. The lioness is an expert at hunting and the highest of hunting power. She is strong, brave, fearless, a protector of the young and team member of the sisterhood of another female lioness.

The lioness is the primary hunter of food for her cubs and for the alpha male lion. The communal is made up of several lionesses and one or two alpha males. The male is there for protection and to keep other lions outside their communal from taking over their territory. Lions are very territorial in the sense that once they stake out an area by urinating, it creates a boundary and no outside lions are expected to cross the lines of demarcation. The lion is there to keep the young male lions in order and, if they must, discipline them; but his primary job is to protect the community. The male lion gets what is called the "lion's share" of the food from the lionesses hunting excursions. He eats first. The lioness and the cubs eat secondly.

The real beauty of watching these sleek, powerful and beautiful creatures is how naturally skilled they are. They have a highly skilled instinct when it comes to hunting and is almost unmatched by any other animals in the animal kingdom. They will risk their lives when it comes to their cubs, taking extreme care that they are always safe. The other amazing thing about the lioness is their bond as a sisterhood and how they lovingly relate to one another. They always work together in groups to hunt for food and care for each other's cubs.

When taking down the buffalo (their favorite choice of food) so there will be enough food for everyone to eat, they skillfully use suffocation as the primary way to kill their prey by covering the mouth, nasal passage, and the throat. By using this method, they cut off all the air passages of their enemies.

The lioness is bold and relentless. She will patiently wait for her prey for hours in the open to give the appearance that she is not interested. But when she rises and feels the timing is right, she is now ready to strike. With the backing of the other females and the trained older cubs, she will take down 500-pound buffalos with no problem. She can outrun the average zebras and gazelles. She can get up to 70 to 80 miles per hour in speed with no real effort. Her eyesight is keen and she has extreme night vision, giving her the advantage over other wild animals.

You, my sister, have the ability to be a lioness woman. You are beautiful, intelligent and strong. You have an inner strength that you have not allowed yourself to tap into. You can rise to the occasion when it comes to the protection of your family and children. God has given you the innate ability to overcome hardships and impossible odds time after time. We have keen insight and can easily discern when there is something going on with our children, our mates, or when something is off emotionally or spiritually in our homes. Sisters, like the lioness, we are better together. We can change the world if we are willing to love and support one another.

We must be willing to cross racial barriers and love other sisters of different cultures. God has made us the same sisters in some of our most basic physical attributes and abilities. As well, He has made the lioness the same in their most basic physical attributes and abilities. We are all females. We are all women. We all nurture and protect. We all have the ability to be Lioness Women.

We can take down the enemies in our communities by cutting off the enemy's air supply of drugs, murders, break-ins, disrespect, and any form of unrest in our communities if we are willing to form a strong bond of sisterhood. We must be willing to love ourselves first and then love each other.

What makes you look bad makes me look bad. When you are disrespected, I am disrespected. When you hurt, I hurt. When you lose, I lose. When you win, I win. My success is not to make you look bad. My success is to give you hope. It is to open the door and to leave it open for you to enlarge your possibilities. I'm your sister. I'm your answer. I'm your hope. I am my sister's keeper. I love you.

Amen Sister!

"And Jabez called on the God of Israel, saying, Oh that thou wouldest bless me indeed, and enlarge my coast, and that thine hand might be with me, and that thou wouldest keep me from evil, that it may not grieve me! And God granted him that which he requested" (I Chronicle 4:10)

The Question Is?

"The Question is: Will I ever leave? Will I do your will? When will Jesus return?"

I love this hit gospel song sung by the Winans. This famous group of brothers from Detroit, Michigan has a long history of hits and this is probably one of my favorites and, in my opinion, one of the most important as it relates to your salvation and your relationship with our Savior Jesus Christ.

Daily, we have to ask ourselves the question: "Are we prepared for Jesus' return?" The Bible says to examine ourselves and see if we be in the faith (2 Cor. 13:5a). If we will judge ourselves, then we won't have to be judged by the Judge of the courts of heaven. God is a just God and He desires that no one would be lost.

How wonderful is that to know that God does not want to punish you. He really wants to save you and use you for His glory. God is a loving God and He so loved you and me that He sent His only begotten Son to die for us. He is not some mean God waiting to pounce on you because you have done wrong, but He wants to love you and to rescue you from your internal scars and battles.

God will not force Himself on you, but He wants you to choose Him like any other lover. He wants to be loved by you. He can and He is willing to comfort you and restore you back to the place that He had for you since the beginning of time. There is no sin that He cannot pardon. He wants to pardon you and set you free.

Have you asked yourself these very important questions? Take some time and reflect. Are you ready for Jesus' return? Are you sure and very sure that your anchor holds and grips the solid rock of Jesus Christ? You can be sure and very sure. Right at this moment, in a twinkling of an eye, you can go from death unto life. Make it a priority to invite Jesus into your life today. He's waiting for you.

The Winans, in this hit song, gave the answers to the questions: No. You (God) will never leave me. Yes. I'll do Your will. You will return soon, soon, soon.

Amen Sister!

> "But of that day and hour knoweth no man, no, not the angels of heaven, but my Father only"
> (Matt. 24:36)

A Kingdom Breaking Through

"Breakthrough"- an offensive thrust that penetrates and carries beyond a defensive line in warfare. An act of overcoming, or penetrating an obstacle or restriction.

The Bible tells us, "And from the days of John the Baptist until now the kingdom of heaven suffereth violence, and the violent take it by force" (Matt. 11: 12). What is a kingdom? It's the government, the rule and the reign of a governing body. So, in God's kingdom, He rules, and reigns. The Bible says "the government is on His (Jesus') shoulders" (Isa. 9:6). We, as kingdom people, have the awesome responsibility to pray until we see change come. We are to pray as the Lord has instructed us to pray, "Thy kingdom come. Thy will be done in earth, as it is in heaven" (Matt. 6:10). We must pray heaven down to the earth. We must pray the will of God to be done in our homes, in our cities, in our countries, and in our nations.

The Bible says Elijah was a man of like passion and he prayed that it did not rain for three years. The heavens were shut up and it did not rain, because of the wickedness of King Ahab and his wife Jezebel. Elijah said to King Ahab, "Now Elijah the Tishbite, who was of the settlers of Gilead, said to Ahab, "As the LORD, the God of Israel lives, before whom I stand, there shall be neither dew nor rain these years, except by my word" (I Kings 17:1AMP).

The heavens did not produce rain and there was famine in the land. There were so much power and passion in Elijah's words, and to think that a man, not God, could shut up the heavens with his words. Elijah prayed again. God heard Elijah's prayers, and the kingdom of God broke through on his behalf, and the heavens produced rain!

We must pray until atmospheres are changed. We are to decree and declare what we want to see happen, not what we see with our natural eyes but with our spiritual eyes. We must ask the "Lord of the breakthrough" to go before us. He is the Lord of the breakthrough.

Jesus is the Breaker. Jesus Christ our Advocate has gone before us on our behalf and He has broken the strongholds of the devil. As I said earlier, if anything is going to get done in the earth we, the people of God, have the power to pray, "Thy kingdom come.
Thy will be done, on earth as it is in heaven." We are the only ones that can pray that prayer. We have a Kingdom that cannot be shaken!

It's time to pray strategic prayers. Prayers that reach the heavens. Too much is at stake. We have too much to lose. God, help us that we don't lose heart and faint. I don't know about you, but I'm ready to see a breakthrough for me, my family, my friends, my church, the people of God, my city, my country, the nations, the president and the leaders of this world. I'm not asking God to bless me, my four and no more. No, no, no that's selfish. I need God to bless others also.

"God, we need your Kingdom to come. We need a breakthrough in our circumstances. Just as you did for Elijah, you can do it for us in our circumstances. There's a drought in the land and we need the rain of the Holy Spirit. There's a drought in my relationships, my circumstances, my marriage, and my finances. Help me to smash down every wall of defense and break through the enemy's line with your unshakeable Kingdom. I need a kingdom break~~through. You are Lord of the breakthrough. Lord, break~through for me. Break~through for my sisters.

Amen Sister!

"Let your kingdom come. Let your will be done, on earth as it is in heaven" (Matthew 6:10)

Journal Notes

"For thine is the kingdom, and the power, and the glory, forever. Amen. (Matthew 6:13)

Discovering Your Roots

As I watched the Alex Haley's movie *Roots*, I wondered if we have given thought regarding our roots and where our ancestry all started? Many of us would go to one of the matriarchs or patriarchs of the family to hear the stories of our forefathers, our great-grandparents, and those that came before us.

My father's family was small and I don't know too much about his family beyond his mother and three sisters and their immediate families. On the other hand, my mother's family was large. There was my grandfather, grandmother, six girls, uncles, cousins and a host of extended family members. I spent many years at my grandmother's house, which we called the "Big House" in River Rouge, Michigan bordering the city of Detroit. Those were very memorable years so much so that I vowed one day I would live in Detroit, Michigan and indeed I did.

Again, the question is: "Have you ever thought about your roots?" I want to go a little deeper than just your family, but I want you to think about your spiritual roots. Do you know that you also have spiritual roots? Our roots began with our first spiritual parents Adam and Eve, all the way to the birth of Jesus Christ.

Your spiritual roots are just as important as your biological roots. You must know that you have a Father who is the Almighty God. You have an Advocate named Jesus who laid down His life for you and we also have a family called the Church. We are related through the Blood of Jesus. The more you know about your spiritual roots the more at peace and the more complete your life will be.

Alex Haley went on a journey of discovery to Africa to find his biological roots and having gone that far he did not go far enough. Our true roots begin in the Garden with God when He said, "Let it be." I thank God for this, my sisters. We can honestly know where we all began and where we will all eventually return. This earthly home is just our temporary home, but we have a home that is not made by hands, brick or mortar it awaits us in heaven.

What are your ancestral roots? Where did your parents come from? I admonish you to take time and go on a journey of discovery to discover where we as humans have come from and it will strengthen you to know you also have spiritual roots and they begin with God the Father in His garden.

Amen Sister!

"So God created man in his own image, in the image of God created he him; male and female created He them. And God blessed them, and God said unto them, Be fruitful, and multiply, and replenish the earth, and subdue it: and have dominion over the fish of the sea, and over the fowl of the air, and over every living thing that moveth upon the earth"

(Gen 1:28)

My Body, His Temple

The Bible asks the question, "Know ye not that your bodies are the members of Christ?" (I Cor. 6:15a). Don't you know you are God's temple?" Do we really know that? Do we really treat our bodies as if they are something sacred? God says we are the temple of the Living God and said, "I will live within them and walk among them" (2 Cor. 6:16). What a powerful statement. But, do we really know and act towards our bodies like we house God's Spirit in our bodies?

How many of us know that there are some wrong things we have put in our bodies and there are some wrong things we have allowed our bodies to come in contact with? God is concerned about every aspect of our lives, our health, and our wellbeing. 3rd John 2:2 says, "Beloved, I pray that you may prosper in all things and be in health, just as your soul prospers."

We must be whole on the inside and outside. The body, mind (soul) and spirit are known as the tri-economy of man and they must be in complete harmony. When we are not well emotionally, it can cause sickness in our bodies. Stress can kill us emotionally and cause physical and physiological disorders.

Our thoughts are very important to our everyday health. The Bible says, "Finally, brethren, whatsoever things are true, whatsoever things are honest, whatsoever things are just, whatsoever things are pure, whatsoever things are lovely, whatsoever things are of good report; if there be any virtue, and if there be any praise, think on these things" (Phil. 4:8).

Why should we think on these things? It is because our thoughts produce healthy bodies. Healthy thoughts are the keys to healthy living. **We are what we eat and we are what we think.**

The human body is an amazing creation. Although our bodies grow and change during the course of our lives, we only get ONE body. This body sees us through from birth to death, so it's important that we properly care for our bodies. Our human body is likened to that of the Ford truck commercial; **"It's built to last,"** but how long it lasts depends on proper maintenance.

Yes, it's your body, but He calls it His temple. If we see our body the way He sees it, we would treat it better. We spend a lot of money on maintaining the body. We exercise, we put pretty clothes on the body, and we buy and drink healthy drinks. We adorn it with the loveliest jewelry and the finest perfume. All of this is good, but the Bible says bodily exercise profits us little (I Tim. 4:8.) Yes, we are to exercise; yes, to all the other things that we do; but that does not make it God's temple. God wants to dwell on the inside of our human spirit and when the Holy Spirit dwells on the inside of our human spirit we become His temple and can now have direct communications to receive instructions from the Almighty God.

Amen Sister!

"Know ye not that ye are the temple of God, and that the Spirit of God dwelleth in you? [17] If any man defile the temple of God, him shall God destroy; for the temple of God is holy, which temple ye are"

(I Cor. 3:16-17)

A Kingdom Woman

A Kingdom Woman is designed by God's hand to rule, reign and take dominion. God has given her the authority to change the atmosphere and the environment around her.

She is a mother, sister, auntie, cousin, friend and, most importantly, a daughter of the "Most High King." A Kingdom Woman is confident, strong, loving, giving and kind.

She is a follower but yet a leader, always willing to lead the way so others may follow. She sets her standards high, but she's always reaching for higher heights and deeper depths. She ain't a joke! She's a real woman. The real deal.

Many are intimidated by her presence, but her presence is the essence of God. She's a cut above the rest because she wants the very best not just for herself but for others also. She is a high impact woman, always setting her mind on those things that are above, yet willing to do whatever her hands find to do here on the earth and to do it with all her might.

She's always encouraging, provoking and lifting up others. She sees potential, the God potential, in others because she's a Kingdom Woman called to make a difference in the Kingdom and in the world.

A Kingdom-minded Woman is always looking for ways to make improvements and she encourages others to improve themselves by being the best they can be. She is a woman full of resources and information, a Kingdom connector, connecting others to their blessing without intimidation, jealousy or competition.

A Kingdom Woman is a woman with a Kingdom-mindset, always tending to the natural and as well as the spiritual things of God and can operate efficiently in both kingdoms. A Kingdom Woman is a businesswoman and yet she is a wife, mother, homemaker, girlfriend and a prayer warrior. She is always teaching, yet she is always learning and willing to teach others. She is a collaborator always willing to join in and help others even if it was not her idea, her event or her business. She is always about the good of others. The Kingdom Woman is a woman, but she is always a lady.

Amen Sister!

"Who can find a virtuous woman? for her price is far above rubies. The heart of her husband doth safely trust in her so that he shall have no need of spoil"
(Proverbs 31:10-11)

The Wounded Heart

Many years ago I had the opportunity to work in the Physical Therapy Department of a medical facility that cared for indigent and geriatric patients. My responsibility was to assist the resident Physical Therapist with gait training, exercising and giving whirlpool therapy to patients with wounds from one source or another. Some of my patients were chronic drug users; some were older patients no longer able to walk and now were bedridden, and some were patients with severe wounds from burns.

Some patients required I give whirlpool therapy with the aid of a Betadine treatment to assist in the healing process of the wound. This would require the doctor to use a scalpel to cut and scrape away dead tissue from the wound because the dead tissue would cause death to the perfectly healthy and living tissue. The dead tissue would be dark and sometimes carry an odor. The circulation of the water and the Betadine treatment would cause the wound to begin to heal and fresh tissue would begin growing in its place.

I remember one of the darkest points in my life. After being divorced for some years, my ex-husband asked me to marry him again. We both were attending church on a regular basis and had spent almost a year in marriage counseling with our pastors. So, I felt this time would be different from the first marriage.

Well, on the rehearsal night, he came late and informed me, my pastors and the wedding party that he was not ready. He stood me up one week before the wedding. I later learned there also was another woman involved. I was devastated, to say the least.

We were encouraged by our pastors to give it some more time, to continue counseling, and see what happens. It was too late. My heart was broken and wounded. It felt like someone had stabbed me in my heart. I was in need of strength, having to inform people the wedding was off. I regretfully made my apologies to my bridal party and went home to make phone calls.

The days turned into nights and the nights seemed as if they were 24 hours long. I would sit and cry and wonder how could this happen to me? It took a long time, but eventually, the wound in my heart began to heal. The medicine was the Word of God, prayer and the love I received from my pastors, friends, and family.

During the time I was going through the healing process, the Holy Spirit began to speak to me about the five stages of a wounded heart. Much unlike a physical wound, a wound in the heart cannot be seen on the outside, but there is a big hole on the inside that is in desperate need of repair. These are the stages:

The first stage of the wounded heart is the **Trauma Stage**: it is at this stage you actually got wounded; the trauma and the devastation. And, at this stage, you can really lose yourself in your pain, hurt, and humiliation or even your mind. This is the most fragile stage.

The second stage is the **Admission Stage**: this is the stage that you must identify the hurt and the pain. You must identify to purify. It is also this stage that you must give yourself the permission to say, "I'M ANGRY!" I HURT! I WANT REVENGE!

The third stage is the **Repentance Stage**: "Lord, forgive me my trespasses as I forgive those that trespass against me. Forgive me for those I may have hurt, as I forgive those who hurt me. I know I must forgive so I can be forgiven. Yes, it hurts. Yes, it was wrong. But I choose to forgive. Now, help me Holy Spirit to forgive. I may not forget, but help me to forgive."

The fourth stage is the **Healing Stage**: This is the stage after the confession and repentance - where the work begins. It is at this stage the day-by-day venting, crying, blaming, screaming, anger and facing all your issues one by one takes place. This is the stage of grappling with God in prayer, reading the word and worshipping. This is the debriding process, the cutting away of the dead tissues and issues in your life.

This is the loneliest and the longest part of the whole process. You feel like Jesus when He was in the Garden of Gethsemane. He was praying, asking the Father if this cup could pass from Him. You want this hurt to hurry up and pass, but the healing process must take place. The scalpel of the Word of God, like a skilled surgeon, must cut away those dead things so you can live a new and fresh life once again.

The fifth stage is the **Healed and Made Whole Stage**:
The storm is finally over! The pain, shame or hurt has subsided and you are beginning to feel your life coming back to you. You can begin to see clearly now that the rain is gone and the storm clouds are passing over. Life seems to be happy, meaningful and with purpose again. You almost thought you were going to die before you got to this stage. You thought you were going to lose your mind, but you made it!!

Now, **Part Two** of this stage is to maintain your healing and maintain your wholeness. You must go through all of the above stages to get to this last stage. And all of those stages were needed and necessary to get you here so you can heal. The goal of any medical treatment plan is to treat and then get your body to begin to heal. That is the same goal and plan God has for us, to get us through our life issues so we can heal and become whole.

The heart, like a physical wound, can and will heal over time. With the right prescription plan and the right treatment plan, we will begin to open up, receive love and trust again. We must keep bitterness, hatred, and forgiveness out at all cost. Anyone of those deadly poisons can cause us to become cold, hard, and callous and can cause septicemia or blood poisoning.

The life is in the blood and our life eternal is in the Blood of Jesus. We must allow the love of God and the Word of God to heal us.

I thank God for what He allowed me to go through and come out on the other side the victor and not the victim. All of the bitterness, anger, and unforgiveness are gone. Now, because of what I have experienced, the Holy Spirit said to me, "You are a Wound Care Specialist."

I am now equipped to care for my sisters so they can heal their wounds and become whole. I can help you and assist you to cut away the dead tissues and scars of your hurt, pain, and past. I can help you by administering the Betadine of the Word of God, the word of wisdom, words of comfort and love to you.

Like the Good Samaritan, I want to pour in the oil and the wine of the Spirit of God, because nothing can heal you like the Spirit of God. He is the Great Physician. He is the Balm in Gilead to heal your wounded heart. I want to see you healed, my sisters. I want to see you whole and I want to see you free. I thank God that I can say today, I am healed. I am whole. I am free. I forgive and I am forgiven.

Amen Sister!

"He heals the brokenhearted and binds up their wounds"
(Ps. 147:3)

Journal Notes

"The Spirit of the Lord God is upon me, because the LORD has anointed me to preach good tidings to the poor. He has sent me to bind up the brokenhearted, to proclaim liberty for the captives and the opening of the prison to them that are bound." Isaiah 61:1

The Perfect Storm

There are times in every life when we will face a storm. That storm in your life is a real storm with seemingly destructive consequences, but it didn't come to destroy you. It came to change you. It's a perfect storm and all the conditions are ripe for change. Everything is in order for you to be changed and at the same time to be blessed.

When you see the storm clouds, don't try to chase them away. Don't try cursing the storm to send it away, because it comes to blow away some things. It comes to shake up some things. It comes to set some things in order in your life. It is the perfect storm.

God knows the velocity of the wind and how long and hard it should blow. He knows what to blow away and what to keep in your life. Everything in your life does not have to be blown away, but there are things that will abort your future and the destiny God has for you.

God knows how much of the storm you can take. He knows when to speak to the storm and when to say, "Peace be still." This storm came to get your attention. It came to say to you, "Be still and know that I am God in your life and your circumstances. Is there anything too hard for God?" No! There is absolutely nothing too hard for God.

God wants you to rest in your storm and allow Him to bring to you the most wonderful plan He has for your life. He can see so much further than you can see. You can be assured that He is on board to guide and navigate you through the storm.

If you stay in the boat, nothing will be lost and you will discover so much about yourself and, more importantly, about Him. Trust Him with your life and with the plans He has awaiting you after the storm has passed over. He is a Great Navigator that knows how to guide you through the storms of life. He will not allow the waters to overtake you. You will not drown. You will stay afloat. You just have to trust Him with all your heart. The storm will pass over. You will get to your destiny. Hallelujah!

Amen Sister!

"Then they cry unto the Lord in their trouble, and he brought them out of their distresses. He stilled the storm to a whisper; the waves of the sea were hushed. They were glad when it grew calm, and he guided them unto their desired haven" (Ps. 107:28-30) NIV.

Minding Your Own Business

Usually, when someone says to you, "Mind your own business," it carries a negative connotation. It usually means that someone thinks you are being too nosey and they don't want to discuss the matter with you. Or, they think you are getting too much into their personal business.

We are in a time and season when we must have more than one plan to provide for ourselves and our families. We must begin to tap into our creativity, which would provide ways to unlock our God-given potential. It is on the inside of us where it always has been and it is time to release it and let it go. When the economy is down, we call it the worst of times. God calls it the best of times. Why? Because these are the times that will force us to go inside of ourselves instead of looking to the outside and pull out what He has placed in us from the beginning.

It is time to go back and dust off those dusty visions, dreams, and goals and begin to do the thing we were created to do. Some of you might have books or music that you have in your mind to write and never took the time to sit down and write. For some, it may be a business idea that we did not take seriously and never got to it. For others, you may want to lose that extra 15-20 pounds and never went on that diet. Well, now is the season to do all those things that you have put on the shelf…just do it!!

How many have good intentions, but never put in the time and planning to "minding your own business?" It's time to do what you were called to do before someone else comes along and does the very thing that God has ordained and assigned to you.

These are seasons of uncertainty and seasons of transition. Everything is changing or is subject to change. The stock market is uncertain, job losses, bank failings, home foreclosures, major business closings. Yes, it is a risk; but what in life isn't a risk, but the risk you must take. You have put time and labor in someone else's dream, someone else's vision, and someone else's business. But what happened to the dream, vision or business God gave to You?

Yes, you may have great success working in another man's dream, but the real fulfillment will come when you do that which you know God has created you to do. When you discover only what He knows is your God-given purpose then and only then will come peace and freedom of prosperity and posterity such as you have never known.

I pray that you will begin your road to discovering, re-discovering and releasing your God-given potential and that you will find the faith and strength to do what you have been wonderfully and fearfully made to do by "minding your own business."

Amen Sister!

"And whatever you do, work at it with all your heart, as working for the Lord, and not human masters"
(Colossians 3:23 NIV)

Your Womb Is Blessed

Many of us have people we admire, desire, or want to emulate. We see the many wonderful things that God is doing in and through their lives and wonder if, "I can be as powerful or as creative as that person?"

We see the Oprah's, the Maya Angelou's, or the Michelle Obamas, or whoever your favorite person is. We wonder, "Can I do that which I see in them? Do I have what it takes to make that kind of impact on others?" Yes, you can. To you, it may sound like a mission impossible. You might think, "I'm not that smart, or I don't have the education or the influence they have or one day I'll to do something like that."

You can't get God's promises through the womb of another. It must be through the womb God has chosen: **your** womb, **your** vision, **your** dreams, **your** goals, and desires must come through God's chosen womb and birth through you. **You** have to do it, not the rich, the famous, the intellectual, and the powerful with all of their seeming circle of influence and their network of people. It must come through **your** womb.

In the 16th chapter of Genesis, God promised Abraham a seed and that he would be the father of many nations as the sands on the seashore. But Abraham allowed himself to agree with Sarah's plan that they would have a child through her handmaiden Hagar's womb. Sarah and Abraham were getting up in age and Sarah thought she may never have a child, though God had made a promise they would have a child and would come from Abraham's loins. This child would be the child of promise and God did, indeed, keep His promise to Abraham. So, Isaac, the child of promise, was born.

The surrogate mother was not able to stop the plan that God had for Abraham. Abraham loved the child and it grieved him when Hagar and the child had to leave because it was causing conflict between him and Sarah. So Sarah had Hagar and the child put out.

Hagar was not able to bring out of her womb the plans that God had for Abraham. God did bless her and the child, but that was not the womb for the child of promise.

It is your womb, the place where God has placed on the inside of you, the business, the ministry, the plans, and purposes that He wants you to birth and bring forth in the earth. Like Sarah, you must birth your vision through your womb. It won't come through the womb of another, such as Hagar. Your vision must be birthed by you.

The earth is waiting for your next idea. It's waiting for your next book, your next ministry, your next plan, the next God-ordained purpose for your life to come through your womb. You are carrying the child of promise, the seed that will bless the world.

Where are you, Sarah? Sarah, come forth and give birth to your child of purpose. Your child of destiny. I command every Sarah to come forth and give birth!

Amen Sister!

"The fruit of your womb will be blessed, and the crops of your land, and the young of your livestock - the calves of your herds and the lambs of your flock."
(Deuteronomy 28:4 NIV)

Shifting Lanes

While I was driving back from Fletcher, Indiana, I noticed a sign posted on the side of the road that said, "Shift Lanes." "Wow," I said out loud. "This is something we all should want to do; shift lanes so we can keep it moving."

We are on this highway called, "Life Under Construction," and there are times when we need to shift lanes. We don't want to leave the highway. We just want to shift lanes so we can continue on in the path and lane that God has for us. We want to shift lanes because we don't want to run into that brick wall or into that construction zone filled with those orange construction barrels. We don't want to hit those potholes and receive a flat tire and have to wait a long time on a tow truck. We have to shift lanes.

Shifting lanes sometimes is not an option. Shifting lanes can save our lives. Is this your season to shift something in your life? Is this the season to move someone or something out of your life? Shifting lanes mean that God is now able to pour something new into your life. Sometimes, before we can get something new, we have to get the old out. We have to shift lanes.

Shifting lanes can be frightening because we have become complacent where we are and not where God wants to take us. Shifting lanes will require something of us; maybe making new friends and meeting new people, maybe going to school, changing jobs or getting out of a relationship that has limited you. But, you must shift to go higher. Otherwise, if you keep on the same path or road that you are on, you will run into that brick wall or that zone of construction that takes you nowhere.

Shift out and away from that construction zone, sisters, so you can keep it moving. Shift out of that fear that keeps you bound to things that are impeding your progress. Shift out of those relationships that are not ordained for your life that keep you stumbling and going into a place of heartbreak and despair. Change gears and make the shift while you have the time and the energy to do what you were put here to do. If you shift and change lanes, you will find that you can breathe easier, you can walk faster, you might find that you can even fly. You can fly. You can touch the sky. You must believe in yourself and begin now to shift lanes into your future.

Amen Sister!

"For with God, nothing shall be impossible"
(Luke 1:37)

Journal Notes

"The name of the LORD is a strong tower: the righteous runneth into it and is safe." (Proverbs 18:10)

The Fragrance of Prayer

You're probably wondering what a fragrance has to do with prayer. Have you ever heard the song *"Sweet Hour of Prayer?"* It is truly a sweet fragrance that lingers on you when you have a consistent prayer life. When a woman spends time in prayer for her marriage, her children, her extended family members, her church or her community, there is a fragrance that comes upon her like a fragrance from a rose because of a woman that dares to kneel in prayer.

The woman is the fragrance of the house during her time and conversations that she has with the Lord on behalf of her family in the Sweet Hour of Prayer. She finds the answers that she needs on how to meet the demands of her family, how to please her husband, and how to have time to be all that God is calling her to be. She can unlock many secrets on how to save money and time in caring for her family; how to make sure her children are safe and spending time with the right people; how to have the career or business, or additional income for her family budget.

When we spend time in prayer and seeking God for answers as the Scriptures tell us, we become the aroma of Christ.
We can attract the right people to us. We can get opportunities given to us that we know we don't deserve nor are we qualified for. We can attract hurting men and women that trust us with their secrets because they can smell the aroma and the fragrance of Christ upon our lives. They don't know that what they are really experiencing is the fragrance of prayer. The fragrance of our worship.

Become a praying woman. Make prayer a daily habit or a priority in your daily lifestyle. Pray and continue to pray until you see something happen. Be determined to see your life and the life of your family changed and surrounded by peace, joy, and prosperity.

It takes sustained prayer and you will walk away with a fragrance that no company or manufacturer can duplicate. It is called The Fragrance of Prayer.

"Sweet hour of prayer. Sweet hour of prayer. That calls me from a world of care. And bids me at my Father's throne. Makes all my wants and wishes known. In seasons of distress and grief, my soul has often found relief. And oft escaped the tempter's snare by thy return, sweet hour of prayer." William Walford (1801-1900)

Amen Sister!

"Then took Mary a pound of ointment of spikenard, very costly, and anointed the feet of Jesus, and wiped his feet with her hair: and the house was filled with the odour of the ointment"
(John 12:3)

Waiting On God

Waiting for anything can be a test of your faith or a test of your will. It's as if when you focus on the thing or situation you are waiting for it just seems to take longer. I heard someone say, "If you are watching a pot of water waiting for it to boil, it seems to take longer for it to reach the boiling point."

The same is the situation if you are waiting on God for an answer. If you are anxious or waiting nervously and stressing over the outcome, then the answer seems to take longer. When we ask God for something, we must first make sure it is according to His will. God's will is His Word. Is the thing you are asking God for according to His Word? God will not violate His Word.

Sometimes we try to bargain with God like the game show "Deal or No Deal." "God, do we have a deal that you are going to do this thing according to my timetable and according to my way? Is that a deal or no deal? Well, God, if I have a choice then let me have this and not that or let me have all of this and I need it by next month. Is that a deal or no deal? Remember, I paid my tithes and offering last month and I helped out in the Nursery. Do we have a deal?"

Now, I know that sounds a little immature but sometimes we try to bargain with God because waiting can get the best of us and waiting can make us weary. "And let us not be weary in well doing: for in **due season** we shall reap, if we faint not" (Gal. 6:9). The problem is that we don't know when or how long the due season is going to take.

You are not alone. If it is any consolation to you, most people don't like to wait or wait too long! Your due season is coming if it is in accordance with the will that God has for your life. His delays are not his denials.

Sometimes He says no to protect us. Sometimes you are not ready for what you are asking, and He says no because He knows it will take you off the pathway He has for you. He knows that hope deferred can make the heart sick, but He knows just at the right time to cause that prayer to manifest. Abba Father knows what is absolutely best for our lives. He knew us from our mother's womb before we ever came into being and He has been with us all of our lives. He promised never to leave us or forsake us. God has not forgotten you.

If you are waiting, keep the faith. Continue to pray and believe that God hears your prayer and the answer will be worth the wait.

Amen Sister!

"Wait on the Lord and be of good courage and he will strengthen your heart. Wait, I say, on the Lord"
(Ps. 27:14)

Reveal Yourself To Me

As I sat on my job one day, God gave me a revelation about the many ways He wants to bless you and I. He showed me a picture of a river that He called the "River of Prosperity" or multiple streams of income. He went on to say, "I did not show you this picture for inspiration. I gave it to you for revelation. I'm trying to reveal myself to you in this picture form not to make you feel good. I'm trying to reveal myself to you in another form, a form unfamiliar to you. Unfamiliar with the way I'm coming to you and unfamiliar with what I desire to give you." He told me that prosperity and wealth were unfamiliar to me.

What He was trying to do was reveal to me that He had something greater, something larger; a place much greater than where I was at the time. It was a wealthy place. He had a plan much greater for me than the current job that I was working on and preparing me for the layoff that was soon to come. God wanted me to look beyond my comfortable borders, but that was unfamiliar to me because a job, a nine to five, was all that I had known. I had worked all my adult life and now God was giving me a different blueprint.

God wants to reveal Himself in ways that are unfamiliar to you. I know it's frightening sometimes when God asks us to do things beyond what we can grasp, but we must trust Him. We know that God's ways are not our ways and His thoughts are not our thoughts. We should be open to however God wants to reveal Himself to us, but most of the time we're not. We are not ready for most of the changes that God requires of us.

The Bible gives an account of two men walking along the road. Jesus appeared and revealed Himself to them in a different form, "And they said one to another, Did not our heart burn within us, while he talked with us by the way, and while he opened to us the scriptures?" (Luke

24:32). They did not recognize Him because they were unfamiliar with Him in his pre-accession state. It was along the way that Jesus revealed Himself.

As you go, as you walk along the way with Jesus, pray that He will reveal Himself to you in a new way and in a new form. It may be in a form that you are unfamiliar with but trust that He is God, sovereign in all His ways. Let your heart burn with the new information He wants to reveal to you. Let your heart burn with allowing Him to take you on a new and exciting journey. Let Him reveal Himself to you. Seek Him while He may be found.

Amen Sister!

"That the God of our Lord Jesus Christ, the Father of glory, may give unto you the spirit of wisdom and revelation in the knowledge of Him"
(Ephesians 1:17)

Living On Purpose

Ministering to numerous single women, I find for many the only way we seem to know how to live our lives on purpose is that we must have a man in our lives. This thought is a diabolical lie from the pit of hell. Yes, God said that is was not good for mankind to be alone, but God intended from the beginning for women to know their purpose.

Esther was a Jewish orphaned girl who was adopted and reared by her cousin Mordecai, brought into the king's palace, won the favor of both the keeper of the harem and favor of the King of Persia. She was chosen from among many other women to become the king's wife because his former wife Vashti had refused to perform before the king and his party of drunken dignitaries. The king, not to be embarrassed, now must look for a woman that "knew her place."

What they were looking for was a woman of that day and culture that would be subservient to her man without a purpose of her own. God took us from the rib of man. We are equal, but we have different roles. God is looking for us to know our place, know our purpose that only He has called us to. Yes, we wear many hats; yes, we play many roles and with all of that, we still have a purpose. If you know your place, you can live life on purpose and love life in your purpose.

Initially, Esther did not know her purpose such as many other women doesn't quite know their purpose. It took cousin Mordecai, who became her mentor and coach, to help her identify the "authentic" purpose God had for her. He said to her, "and who knoweth whether thou art come to the kingdom for such a time as this?" (Esther 4:14).

The first enemy we must fight to achieve our purpose is fear. Fear wants to keep us from living life on purpose. Esther was afraid to go before the king because it could cost her life; she risked her life and got an audience with the king.

If you are going to get to your purpose, it is going to cost you something. You are going to have to leave some things to get to your purpose. You might have to leave some friends, family members, places you use to hang out in, and some of your old habits. If you want to see the King of Kings and the Lord of Lords, it will cost you something. Are you willing to risk all and forsake all?

You must identify the "Hamans," the enemies in your life. Haman was an enemy of the Jews and he wanted to annihilate the Jewish race. Who is trying to annihilate you, the destiny and purposes God has for you? Get rid of the Hamans; get rid of the life of compromise. Get rid of those so-called friends that keep lying to you, saying you're okay just the way you are. The Hamans in your life must die!

Get the favor of the King in your life. God's loving-kindness is better than life itself. His love and His favor will open doors for you that no man can shut. You don't have to compromise when you have the favor of God operating in your life.

Living a life that is pleasing to God will cause you to have favor. His favor will take you places you have never been, live in houses that you can't afford, drive a car knowing that your credit is bad and you drive away with that car anyway. He will give you that promotion without the degree. His favor is better than money. His favor is better than life.

My sister, discover your purpose and watch your life take on new meaning. If you need help, get someone to coach you and help you find your authentic self. Live your life on purpose and love your life in your purpose. You have been called into the Kingdom for such a time as this.

Amen Sister!

"The blessings of the Lord maketh rich, and he addeth no sorrow with it"
(Proverbs 10:22)

"Above all else, guard your heart, for everything you do flows from it."
(Proverbs 4:23)

"For where your treasure is there your heart will be also."
(Matthew 6:21

Journal Notes

"For I know the plans I have for you," declares the L*ORD, "plans to prosper you and not to harm you, plans to give you hope and a future" (Jeremiah 29:11)*

A Womb or A Tomb

Jesus' tomb on resurrection morning became a womb the Father God used to birth resurrection life. Death went into the tomb, but life came out. Cursing went in, but life came out of that tomb. The word says, "Cursed is everyone who is hanged on a tree" (Gal. 3:13b). A tomb is a place of burial, a vault; grave; a place where the dead lie. A womb is a place of development, a place where anything is engendered or brought to life. Jesus asked the women coming to the tomb to anoint the body from decay, "Why seek ye the living among the dead?" (Luke 24:5b). It was not His tomb, but it became a womb. It became a place of blessing, a place of birthing. It is a place of bringing forth life.

Women, in the natural sense, have been given by the Creator a womb. We are to be life-givers. We are the man with the womb, called Wo-Man. Our womb should be used for the correct purpose, to birth and bring forth life. It should be the place of developing life, the very essence of man. It should not be used to kill purpose; it should be used to birth purpose. It should be pure and not defiled. It should be clean and not used as a place for men to dump their filth on you. Is your womb a place of un-forgiveness and bitterness that you spew out on others and kill with your words instead of bringing forth life? Are you holding people in prison in this vault, this tomb? If so, this wonderful place that was meant to bring forth life is being used as a place of death.

Each time you have sex outside of the plan of God, outside of marriage, it's a place of death; it becomes a tomb, not a womb. Filth goes in and filth comes out. Yes, you may birth a child there, which is a blessing from God, but what else has been deposited?

More death than life has been left there; more hatred than love; more low-esteem than self-esteem and confidence; and more unforgiveness than forgiveness. What kind of possible diseases has been deposited there? How much shame and confusion have been deposited there?

When we don't know and understand a purpose of a thing we can misuse it for the wrong purpose. Our womb was meant to be clean and reserved for our husbands. You may need a Dilation and Curettage, better known as a D and C, a procedure that is used to scrape the wound to rid it of its impurities after an abortion or miscarriage. Have you miscarried the plans of God for your womb? Is your womb being used for the original purpose that God has for it? Have you aborted the plans He has for the other person by using your womb and making it a tomb?

Well, the good news is that God is a God of restoration. He can and will forgive us and restore us back to the original purpose that He meant for our wombs. No, we can't go back to the state of innocence we've had before we abused our wombs. But, He is a God of a second chance and He will cleanse us and restore us and allow our wombs to become a place of blessing, a place of life and not death.

Let Him give you a spiritual D and C. Let him scrape and cut away from that womb all the impurities that have been left there by sin. Let Him wash you and make you clean that you may have a clear conscience and live your life in peace and joy in the Holy Ghost. He is a God of restoration. He's just waiting for you.

Amen Sister!

"As they entered the tomb, they saw a man dressed in a white robe, sitting on the right side, and they were alarmed. Don't be alarmed he said, you are looking for Jesus the Nazarene, who was crucified. He has risen! He is not here. See the place where they laid Him."
(Mark 16:5-6 NIV).

God I'm in A Crisis

One day as I was complaining to the Lord, "God, I'm in a crisis!" I was in a tight financial crisis at the time due to a slowing down in the automobile industry. I was selling cars and the economy had begun to go into a financial recession. I had stopped to get some gasoline and with 13 cents left and tears in my eyes again I said, "God, I'm in a crisis!" The sweet voice of the Lord spoke to me and said, "My people are never in a crisis." I said to the Lord, "You don't understand. I am REALLY in a crisis! I have 13 cents left in my pocket with no idea where I'm going to get any money before my next paycheck. I am in a crisis!"

What exactly is a crisis? A crisis is defined as a decisive or critical moment. It can be a time of great danger or difficulty, or an emotionally stressful event or traumatic change in a person's life.

The Lord said to me, "I will bring you to the crisis but, I won't leave you in the crisis. You are never in a crisis because you don't know what I'm working out for you. It may look like a crisis to you but it's not a crisis to me." By this time, I'm crying real tears. I reach home, went to my mailbox, and to my surprise there was a $100.00 check in the mail. Well, that $100.00 check looked like a million dollars to me. It may not have been what I wanted, but it was what I needed. I had to ask God for forgiveness for my lack of faith.

God confirmed to me that while I was calling He was answering. You are never in a crisis. Yes, you may be in a tight place at this time but we don't know what the next moment may bring. There is nothing too hard for God to work out in your situation. What may seem like a problem to you is no problem for Him. All He wants is for us to trust Him. You may be thinking, "Linda, you don't understand." Yes, I do understand.

I know sometimes it seems you are backed against the wall with no way out and you wonder how this is going to work out.

I was low on cash before I got down to thirteen cents, but the $100 check was already in the mail. I didn't know that, but God did. He had already had the answer before I could ask the question. He is a God that answers our prayers, our petitions, and even our complaints. He loves you; He loves me, and He is concerned about those things that concern us. He's concerned when he sees the waters of life and adversities about to overtake us and He throws us a lifeline so we won't drown.

Keep holding on; keep believing; keep praying; keep praising. He will come through for you. He won't leave you in the shape you are in. He wants to be your Daddy, your Provider, and your Friend. You have a Friend that sticks closer than any brother or sister.

Amen Sister!

"Can a woman forget her nursing child, and not have compassion on the son of her womb? Surely they may forget, yet I will not forget you"
(Isaiah 49:16)

The Power of a Praying Man

There are a few accounts in the Bible that show us what happens when a praying man prays for his wife. There is power in a man that is submitted to God and has a powerful prayer life. There also is an example of how God will hinder a man's prayer life according to how he deals with his wife.

In Genesis 25:21, the Bible gives the account of Isaac when he was forty years old and married Rebekah. She brought comfort to him after the death of his mother. The Bible says, "And Isaac intreated the LORD for his wife because she was barren: and the LORD was intreated of him, and Rebekah his wife conceived."

Isaac knew the power of prayer and the only way to get his plea satisfied; he needed an answer from God. The LORD heard his earnest plea for his wife. No place in that passage does it say Rebekah prayed. It says that Isaac pleaded with the Lord for his barren wife and she conceived. Isaac was fervent in his praying to the LORD. He wanted children by his wife because he loved her and he wanted children as his inheritance. Isaac birthed through his prayers twins Esau and Jacob who became the father of the 12 tribes of Israel.

The second account is the story of Zacharias and Elizabeth who had no children because Elizabeth was barren and they were well advanced in age. An angel of the Lord appeared to Zacharias and said to him, "But the angel said unto him, Fear not, Zacharias: for thy prayer is heard; and thy wife Elisabeth shall bear thee a son, and thou shalt call his name John" (Luke 1:13).

You can see how powerful and effective the prayers of a righteous man or husband can turn the heart of God. Zacharias's prayers birthed one of the foremost prophets of all times, the forerunner of Jesus Christ, named John the Baptist. This is an example of what kind of mate a woman should desire, a man that knows God and knows how to get in touch with God on his wife's behalf. Barrenness in those days was serious and a disgrace to women that did not bear children.

The husband is the priest of the home; the main prayer warrior for his wife, children, and his home. God has given him the charge to provide and protect his home as to what goes in and what goes out. He is the gatekeeper. As women, we must desire and ask God to give us this kind of man that will have His heart and His ear. When you are sick, or your children in trouble or finances are low and you are looking for answers, that man can get before God and pray in the provisions of his home. Wow! What a relief it takes off you and me when we have a praying man in our life taking charge and taking control. There is power given to the man willing to take on the challenge and pray for his wife and family. Also, there is such unity when a husband and wife will pray together. The Bible says it is in unity that God commands blessings. The unity of the husband and wife praying together will bring the blessing of God in your marriage and in your home.

My sisters, don't be afraid to ask God for a praying man. Dare to ask for a man that will have God's heart and have His ear. In times of trouble, you need more than empty promises. You need someone that will pray on your behalf. You need someone that is genuinely concerned about you and our children. There is power in the power of a praying man.

There is a saying, "Little prayer, little power. Much prayer, much power. No prayer, no power." I choose much prayer and much power. Let the power of your man praying for you, your children or future children, be the power of God's love permeating your home.

"The effectual fervent prayer of a righteous man availeth much" (James 5:16)

Marred by Life

There are circumstances in our lives that can sometimes get the best of us. Life can seem at times so unfair. Life is for the living and the only way to experience life is you have to live it. You live your life one day at a time, hour by hour, minute by minute and second by second. You can have the best-laid plans and sometimes those plans seem to get derailed or they don't happen at all. Some occurrences can cause you to lose hope, faith, and confidence waiting for things you want to see happen which could possibly bring you a better quality of life.

Sometimes in the wait, we get impatient and we try stimulants and things that take us down a broad and darken path. We can get so far off the pathway of life that we wonder if we will make it back to safety. We can become marred or messed up by the life and the choices we have chosen for ourselves.

What exactly is marred? It means something is damaged, disfigured, scarred, injured or blemished by injury or rough wear. Some relationships or circumstances in our lives have left its mark on us emotionally, physically or spiritually and sometimes we can never be the same. Some things we should have never experienced, some places we should have never gone, and some people we should have never met. This is why God said, "handle not, taste not, touch not."

But, there is hope in Jeremiah 18:4, he shows us the example of the potter and the clay. He said, "And the vessel that he made of clay was marred in the hand of the potter: so he made it again another vessel, as seemed good to the potter to make it."

God, the Potter, can take that marred and scarred life of sin, hurt, and pain and make it again into another vessel as it seemed good to Him. He can make a vessel of honor and of good use fit for the Master's Hand. It's not too late and you haven't gone too far for His Hand to reach you right where you are.

The Potter did not throw the clay away. He used the same clay to make a brand new vessel. In this same way God, the Potter, takes our lives and does not throw us away. He still wants to use us because we are usable material. I have friends that have been victims of drug use, prostitution, alcohol, and other stimulants. I have used some of these stimulants at one time or another in my life just to help me make it through whatever life circumstances I felt I was not strong enough to deal with. The stimulants can come in the form of sex, adultery or even homosexuality to cover the pain of rape, incest, molestation, abandonment, adoption, betrayal or divorce. One or all of these things can leave you emotionally, physically or spiritually marred and messed up.

The good news is in verse six, the Potter said, "As the clay is in the potter's hand, so are you in my hand." You and I are in His Hands. Yes, we have gone through some tough spots in life but He is our loving Father and a God of many chances. He wants to take all of our scars and turn them into stars. He wants us to take all of our pain and triumph over every trial and tribulation that we have experienced in life and to know we have victory. We are not defeated. We are victors and not victims.

You are beautiful, my sister, no matter what has taken place in your life. All of life's circumstances come as a teacher and we are the students. We took our courses and now we must pass the test.

Amen Sister!

"But now, O LORD, thou art our father; we are the clay, and thou our potter; and we all are the work of thy hand" (Isaiah 64:8)

Journal Notes

"Hear, O LORD, when I cry with my voice: have mercy also upon me, and answer me" (Ps. 27:7).

"We Need Sisters"

A young wife sat on a sofa on a hot humid day, drinking iced tea and visiting with her mother. As they talked about the responsibilities of life, about marriage, and the obligations of adulthood, the mother clinked the ice cubes in her glass thoughtfully and turned a clear, sober glance upon her daughter.

"Don't forget your Sister," she advised, swirling the tea leaves to the bottom of her glass. "They'll be more important as you get older. No matter how much you love your husband, no matter how much you love your children you may have, you are still going to need sisters. Remember to go places with them now and then; do things with them. And remember that "Sisters" also means your girlfriends, your daughters, and other women relatives, too.
You'll need other women. Women always do."

"What a funny piece of advice!" The young woman thought. "Haven't I just gotten married? Haven't I just joined the couple's world? I'm now a married woman, for goodness sake! A grown up. Surely my husband and the family we may start will be all I need to make my life worthwhile!" But she listened to her mother. She kept in contact with her Sisters and made more women friends each year.

As the years tumbled by, one after another, she gradually came to understand that her mom really knew what she was talking about. As time and nature work their changes and their mysteries upon a woman, Sisters are the mainstays of her life. After over 50 years of living in this world, here is what I've learned:

> Times passes.
> Life happens.
> Distance séparâtes

Children grow up.
Love waxes and wanes.
Hearts break.
Careers end.
Jobs come and go.
Parents die.
Colleagues forget favors.
Men don't call when they say they will.

But, Sisters are there, no matter how much time and how many miles are between you. A Sister is never farther away than needing her can reach. When you have to walk that lonesome valley, and you have to walk it for yourself; your Sisters will be on the valley's rim for you, intervening on your behalf, and waiting with open arms at valley's end. Sometimes, they will even break the rules and walk beside you. Or come in and carry you out.

My sisters, sisters-in-law, and girlfriends, bless my life! The world couldn't do without them, and neither could I. When we began this adventure called womanhood, we had no idea of the incredible joys or sorrows that are ahead, nor do we know how much we would need each other. Every day, we need each other. We need Sisters!

~Author Unknown~

no copyright infringement intended

"My Father", she replied, "you have given your word unto the LORD. Do to me as you have promised, now the LORD has avenged you of your enemies, the Amorites." But grant me this one request," she said. "Give me two months to roam the hills and weep with my friends, because I will never marry." From this comes the Israelite tradition that each year the young women of Israel go out four days to commemorate the daughter of Jephthah the Gilead."
(Judges 11:36-39)

How Does Your Garden Grow?

There is an old Mother Goose nursery rhyme that goes like this: *"Mary, Mary quite contrary. How does your garden grow?"*

When you don't attend or care for your garden, you will begin to produce weeds, thorns, and thistles. There are different kinds of weeds. Some weeds are low to the ground; others grow tall and they even have pretty flowers on them of different colors and assortments, but you know you did not plant them; they just begin to grow. You didn't deliberately place them in the ground; they just came up on their own.

One day while watering my grass and after closely examining some weeds I had never seen before I pondered, "How did they get here?" These weeds were thick, ugly and stubborn looking. I asked myself again, "How did they get here?"

The weeds had some leaves and at the end of the stem was a flower, but it was also ugly. I did not like the way it looked. I said to myself, "This has got to go!" The stem was so thick and heavy it could not stand straight up and caused the plant to bend and grow forward. Ugh! I hated what I saw.

After tugging and pulling this plant, I realized I would have to actually cut this with a knife because it was so stubborn. I could not pull the root up. I had to dig it up. I knew that I had to get the root out of the ground so this plant would not come back again.

How did these weeds come about? Where did they come from? How long had they been there? These weeds came about by not attending my garden. They came about by not taking the time to plant something in that spot, so a weed decided to come in that space.

Planting takes time and care. Planting is planned, thought out and deliberate. I had not attended to my garden and the plants would soon be run over by those ugly weeds. Weeds just seem to come out of nowhere. One day you look and they are just there.

How did they get there? Who planted those weeds? Some can look so nice and innocent, but they are still weeds. Don't let them fool you! That one plant or weed looked plain evil, wicked and hard. It looked as if it was saying to me, "You can't just pull me up. You are going to have to work to get me up." It was a bully plant, but it had to go! It would not come up nice and easy. This plant had to go under the knife.

Sometimes, we have to exam ourselves and ask, "Where have I allowed weeds to grow in my garden?" You are the planting of the Lord. God has planted us by His spirit in this beautiful garden of life. His plans for us are that we would grow into a beautiful plant bringing beauty to the lives around us.

Our lives should give off life and light that others in darkness may be able to see the light in our light. We must check each and every day to see what kind of weeds are growing in our hearts, the seat of our emotions and affections. Am I mean and ugly? Do I have a bitter and unforgiving spirit? Do I draw or do I repel others away from me? Weeds, weeds, weeds.

Well, after careful examination of my garden, I decided I don't like those ugly weeds. I want a beautiful, colorful and sweet smelling garden. I intend to exam my garden more often. I also intend to exam my heart more often and make sure there are no ugly unruly weeds or anything that would keep me from being beautiful and all that God intended me to be. My heart must be weed free and full of light and love.

Amen Sister!

"The seed falling among the thorns refers to someone who hears the word, the worries of this life and the deceitfulness of wealth choke the word and making it unfruitful" (Matthew 13:22 NIV)

Surely, the LORD, you bless the righteous; you surround them with your favor as with a shield. (Psalm 5:12)

For the LORD God is a sun and shield; the LORD bestows favor and honor; no good thing does He withhold from those whose walk is blameless. (Psalm 84:11)

The Fruit Bowl Concept

One day, I was looking at this beautifully decorated fruit bowl with fruits of every kind. There were bananas, oranges, grapes that were red, green, and purple, there were brightly colored apples, pears, pineapples, etc. They were so colorful and arranged so beautifully.

As I stood there looking at that fruit bowl, I said to myself, "Wow! "This is so beautiful and this is how we as women look when we bring all our fruits of gifts and talents together and put them into one bowl.

Each fruit has its own distinct taste, touch, smell, and color. Each fruit has its own distinct shape and form. Some are hard and some are soft; some you peel and some you can just bite into right away. But, each one serves the same purpose: they feed, satisfy and edify us.

God did not intend for us to be alone, or to be an island all to ourselves. Who can see your beauty? Who can know the value of your fruit if you are abiding alone? How can you enhance someone else's life if you are not a part of the fruit bowl concept? You can't, because you are isolated, alone, not enhancing or either being enhanced by someone else's life and the fruit which is in their life.

We each have gifts, talent, ideas and concepts that we need to share with each other. My life experiences and my testimony can be the deliverance or the answer for someone else in need of love, deliverance or answers. We should never think that what we have to share is insignificant or not helpful to someone else. You have value and you matter.

I appeal to you sisters. Let's begin to put all of our fruit into the fruit bowl and begin to appreciate and savor the fruit that is in the heart of the women that God has placed in our lives. Together, we can build something. We can help other women. We can help our communities. We can help our children. We are better together.

My sister, put your fruit in the bowl next to mine. Let's enhance each other, and other sisters that need what we have to offer by becoming a blessing to her. Our gifts, our talents, our ministries, our businesses, our churches are the fruits that beautify the fruit bowls of life.

Amen Sister!

"Every branch in me that beareth not fruit he taketh away: and every branch that beareth fruit, he purgeth it, that it may bring forth more fruit"

(John 15:2)

You Are a Masterpiece

A "masterpiece" refers to a creation that has been given much critical praise, especially one that is considered the greatest work of a person's career, or a work of outstanding creativity, skill or workmanship." (Wikipedia)

There are many notable people that created a masterpiece in their lifetime such as, Mozart's last piano concert Requiem was considered a masterpiece, and Martin Luther King's "I Have a Dream" speech was hailed as a masterpiece. Michelangelo's painting of the Sistine Chapel in the Vatican took four years to complete was considered a wonderful masterpiece. There are many others in every walk of life that have created masterpiece works of some sort. But, the greatest masterpiece is God's creation. The man gives seed to a woman. The woman gives life to the world. The woman was created from the man, and the man is born of a woman. God did not make us as He did Adam from the dust of the earth. He took us from the man's flesh and bone to symbolize in marriage how the two become one flesh.

After the woman became bone of man's bone and flesh of man's flesh it was then that God's creative works were done. And now the woman has become the mother of all living. How awesome is that!

You are the masterpiece of all creation. You must see that for yourself. Say that to yourself. "I am a masterpiece and I was created by the hand of God." He fashioned and designed you to be the unique person that you are. There is no one, absolutely no one, like you. You are a designer original. You are much more than a Gucci bag, Louis Vuitton piece of luggage, or a pair of Louboutin's red bottom shoes. You are priceless you are a rare Masterpiece!

You were created by the Creator of all creators, the Designer of all designers, the Great Creator Himself and He loves you. A masterpiece of a great price. You can put the most expensive clothes on your back, the most expensive shoes on your feet, but if you don't see yourself as priceless you don't appreciate in value, you begin to depreciate and devalue God's creation.

The value is in the creation, not in what is put on it externally. It's what's internal. Add value to God's creation by knowing and respecting who you are. See yourself as God sees you.

You are a Masterpiece!

Amen Sister!

"And God said, Let us make man in our image, after our likeness: and let them have dominion over the fish of the sea, and over the fowl of the air, and over the cattle, and over all the earth, and over every creeping thing that creepeth upon the earth. So God created man in his own image, in the image of God created he him; male and female created he them"
(Genesis 1:26-27)

Journal Notes

I will praise thee; for I am fearfully and wonderfully made: marvelous are thy works; and that my soul knoweth right well. (Psalm 139:14).

Obey The Stop Signs

While driving my car one day, I approached a cross street, the driver to my left had the stop sign but didn't stop. She just kept going. I slowed down, allowing her to cross the intersection to avoid an accident. I thought to myself, "How many times in our lives have we disobeyed or ignored the stop signs?"

Wow! How different things might have turned out if I had only obeyed the stop signs or warnings in my life. How many crashes and disappointments I could have avoided if I only had obeyed my gut feelings that were trying to relay messages to my brain. Messages such as slow down. Don't turn down that street. Watch out! This is a construction zone. This is the wrong way. Don't go that way. This is a dead-end street. God says, "You are at the cross-section and I'm about to do something for you. Just wait!"

Why don't we obey the stop signs? We are disobeying the law when we don't obey the stop signs. We think, "Oh, no one is looking. Oh, I can handle this. I can make it through the stop sign without an accident." But, can we really?

Let's be honest. We really didn't make it through without an accident. The accident of our lives, our choices and our bad behavior, has cost us a lot of time, money, patience and emotions. It would have been so much simpler if I would have stopped, looked and listened.

We don't understand that disobeying stop signs can cost us our very lives. How many situations we can look back on and see God delivering us from hurt, harm, and danger. Stop signs are there to protect us and for the protection of others. When we do disobey the stop signs, we are not just breaking the civil laws we are also breaking God's law.

It is not His desire that we would break His laws or disobey Him when He gives us instructions. And, yes, there are consequences for our disobedience. We all fall short of God's glory once in a while, but it should be our desire to obey Him the first time to avoid the accidents or the head-on collision.

But, the good news is that God is a forgiving Father and He is faithful and just to forgive you. He loves you and He wants what's best for your life just like any natural parent. He wants you to live and to live life more abundantly.

When you find yourself at a crossroad in life, ask the Father which way should you go? Wait for His answer that He may guide you and lead you in the right pathway.

Amen Sister!

"And Samuel said, Hath the Lord as great delight in burnt offerings and sacrifices, as in obeying the voice of the LORD? Behold, to obey is better than sacrifice, and to hearken than the fat of rams"

(I Samuel 15:22)

What Is Your Passion

What is your passion? This is a question I believe every person asks at least once in their lifetime. What do you like to do? What do you believe you were put here on earth to do? What are you good at? What brings you fulfillment?

These are questions that you and only you can answer. If you don't know, spend some time alone in a quiet place and begin to write down some of the things you like to do, starting with the one you like the most. It's okay if you change your mind as you go down the list; the main thing is to do the list.

Life doesn't go in a straight line. It has its highs and lows and ups and down. It is forever evolving and changing like the seasons. So, what you might like today as you go along you may find that this is not what you want to do after all and that's alright.

You have to find your life's current and go with the flow. Your flow might not be someone else's flow, but it's your flow and it flows with who you are. If you try to fight the current and where it is taking you, you will find there are resistances in that flow. That current might not fit you and you seem to be in a struggle trying to fit in. What you have to discern is whether or not this is the right choice or the right fit for me, or maybe I need to go back to the drawing board.

When you find that flow, that right current, you will know it. You will find happiness. You will feel complete. It will wake you up in the morning and you'll enjoy doing what you're passionate about doing. How many people do you know that are miserable, because they have not found that one thing that gives them fulfillment?
Your passion could be your purpose and your purpose could be your passion.

God created us all for a purpose. You are not an accident, no matter what the circumstances surrounding your birth. You have a purpose. When we begin to live on purpose and not by default, life will have so much meaning and you will begin to feel whole and complete. When you do this, you will be living for the purpose of why you are here on earth and your passions for what you are created to do will become your life. And life will become sweeter.

Amen Sister!

"Whatever your hands find to do, do it with all your might."
(Ecclesiastes 9:10 NIV)

Remove The Clutter

As women, we have so much going on in our lives and on our plates. Most of us are good at multi-tasking at more than one thing. We are wives, mother, sisters, aunties, grandmothers, ministers, businesswomen, students, and the list goes on and on.

God has gifted us to have a baby on one hip, talk on the phone and run the vacuum at the same time. We can bring home the bacon and cook it too! Sometimes we become superwoman or like the popular song by Chaka Khan, "I'm Every Woman."

Let's be honest. We can't do everything, nor should we be expected to do everything. We can do some things well, but we cannot do everything. More important is what God expects.

We have to watch this. As women, we are so diverse, gifted and so talented because that's the way God created us and we can become tired and burned out from all the extra-curricular activity. We must remove the clutter in our lives so we can make room for God's blessings and find time to hear what He wants for our lives.

We have to remove the clutter of friends that mean us no good or just taking up all our time. We must remove old and bad relationships that are going nowhere and causing us to keep going around in a circle. We have to remove the clutter from the now attention grabber called the Internet, television and all the media sights.

That does not mean that we have to cut ourselves off from the outside world entirely, but we must monitor what we watch, what we do, what we hear, and who we spend our time with. We are all guilty of this, including me, but we must have quiet time and listen to that still small voice on the inside of us giving us our directions for that moment, day or week.

Our families, friends, church, businesses and our very lives are dependent upon us doing these things. We have to remove the clutter to receive the blessings God has for us.

Some days I plan to do nothing, just spend time thinking, planning, reading my word and hearing from God. I ask God, "What is your next plan for me? What do you want for my life, because it's really your life?" I want to be in the center of His will and when I am not my world is off center; it's tilted and slanted and things just don't seem to fit. They just don't seem to work.

My Sisters, we have to do some spring cleaning and remove what is cluttering up our lives and begin to do what is important to God, our families and to us. God can't get more to us if we are all plugged up with clutter. Our minds are so full of clutter sometimes we can't think or hear straight. We need to break from all outside external forces and get still. Our hearing is off because we are so plugged up and we wonder why we can't hear from God.

We can't solve everybody's problems. Removing the clutter means we have to stop allowing other people's problems to become our problems and be in a place and a space to receive the instructions that God has for us so we can be a blessing in the earth.

So, get your clutter box out and begin to unload and throw out old clothing, old furniture, old broken jewelry, old pictures, broken relationships and things that you no longer have a need for and watch how God will begin to give you replacements for all that has been plugging you up and weighing you down. Go ahead, remove the clutter and make room for the blessing. He wants to bless you, but you must be ready to receive.

Amen Sister!

He says, "Be still, and know that I am God: I will be exalted among the heathen, I will be exalted in the earth" (Ps. 46:10)

The Game Changer

Life can have its ups and down for us all, and life is changing all the time. I was listening to this newest CD by Johnny Gill. Yes, I still like some R&B songs that sing about love and songs having good lyrics. The music of my day and era were love songs or songs that made you want to dance and be free. Yes, some of that music gave you the blues, too, because the lyrics were sad or about someone that you lost or were losing. Anyway, the music of my era was, for the most part, good music.

The song by Johnny Gill, "The Game Changer," is about a man that was carousing around with women, breaking hearts and playing games. One day this particular woman comes into his life and she just turned things around for him and changed his "game." He finally met someone that meant more to him than his playing around. She changed his life. He fell in love with this woman and she took him by surprise and he willingly turned in his "player's card" and stopped his playing games and carousing around. He is really congratulating her and thanking her for what she has done in his life, and he gave it all up for her.

I know women that are happily married or in a relationship can identify with that special man who one day walked into their lives and changed their whole life around. I pray that it's for the better and it makes you happy because love is a beautiful thing if it is with the right person.

Waiting for the right person is so important. So many of us have had multiple relationships that have left us feeling lonely and empty. Yes, waiting for the right person is easier said than done, but it can be done. It takes a conscious decision to say, "I want the best that God has for me. And seconds will not do." I don't want to be someone's side chick or just someone you spend time with when you get around to it. I've been there and no matter how you try to pretend you don't mind and you can deal with it, you are lying to yourself. No one wants to feel they are not worthy of all the love and attention a man can give to you and you to him.

Yes, sometimes sisters, it's not the man; sometimes it's you. You can be the one that needs to turn in your "player card" and stop breaking hearts. Sometimes we hurt others because we've been hurt. Hurting people have a tendency to hurt others.

We must heal from all our past hurts and pain before we can truly love others and truly have a forgiving heart, forgiving others, asking to be forgiven, and allowing love to flow freely through us.

In my life, I found the game changer for me was when Christ came into my life and changed my very life. He truly was the game changer for me. I no longer felt the need to be accepted or validated by someone else. I learned to love myself first. Self-love is a wonderful thing. If you can't love self, you can't possibly love someone else. You must know you deserve someone to love you and care for you. You deserve the best. You are worth it and worthy of true love.

Christ can and wants to be the Game Changer for your life. He loves you and wants the very best for your life now and in the future. Just let the "Game Changer of Life" change your life and give you the life you have never experienced. He is the Ultimate Game Changer.

Amen Sister!

"Hereby perceive we the love of God, because he laid down his life for us: and we ought to lay down our lives for the brethren"
(1 John 3:16)

Journal Notes

"Casting all your care upon Him: for He careth for you."
(1 Peter 5:7)

Too Much Power

Power can be dangerous in the hands of a person that does not know how to use it for the right reasons. Many people want power or to be in a position of power and are not fully ready for the responsibility that comes with that power. Yes, power carries a responsibility. A gun in the hands of a wrong person lacking the responsibility that goes with that much power can be very dangerous.

Being a former automobile saleswoman for a Chrysler dealership, I learned while on a test drive with someone not accustomed to driving a car with high horsepower can be very scary. It could cost your life and all you're trying to do is sell a car.

As I was driving one day, there approached me on my right-hand side a Dodge Challenger RT. This particular car is one with high horsepower. The RT has a Hemi engine that is loaded with 5.7 V-8 engine and 375 horsepower. Wow! This car is designed for the car enthusiast. The engine has a roar that will make you turn your head as it passes you by and leaves you in the dust. And, there is another model called the Hellcat with a 6.2 Liter V-8 engine with 707 horsepower!! That is too much power!

Some people are power struck and they love having titles. They feel that having a position gives them the authority to say and do what they could not ordinarily. They hide behind their titles and lord over people or become demanding because they have power. That is too much power.

When God promotes us, we must carefully use the position of power He has given us to be a blessing to others. We must not forget where the power came from. The Bible says, "For promotion cometh neither from the east, nor from the west, nor from the south" (Ps. 75:6).

No matter what position you have when the promotion comes, yes, you did the work, but God does the promoting. If you continue to do the work, in spite of what others may say or think, God will continue to promote you. Sometimes our promotion may not be in a job. It may be God wanting to stretch you into entrepreneurship.

When God gives us an opportunity to speak for Him, whether in ministry or in the marketplace, we must be aware of the power that comes with that position. Many people have been damaged because we have used our power in the wrong way. We must use this power to do good and not evil.

Amen Sister!

"Then he answered and spake unto me, saying, This is the word of the Lord unto Zerubbabel, saying, Not by might, nor by power, but by my spirit, saith the Lord of hosts"
(Zechariah 4:6)

My Center

The late great singer Ella Fitzgerald sang a song called, *Into Each Life, Some Rain Must Fall.* We all know that life has its ups, downs, twist, and turns. One day can bring the sunshine and the next day it's raining cats and dogs, so to speak. Well, that is the interesting thing about life; there's never a dull moment.

Life definitely has its precious moments and unforgettable memories we make as we have opportunities to enjoy our families, take vacations or welcome new family members into the world. These are precious and happy moments.

We all would love to have these memories last forever: those type of situations that are peaceful, joyful and without any major drama. How boring life would be! We all need a little drama. It spikes up our lives.

When I have those seasons in my life, and my boat is rocking and reeling, the bottom seems to have dropped out, and I've come to the end of self, I have to run to my "center." I have to run to safety. He is my strong tower I can run in and be safe. There are sometimes you can't walk but you have to run for shelter. The shelter of his arms.

My center is prayer and seeking God. He is the one that gives me courage. He is the one that steadies my boat when it's rocking. He is the one I have to look to for answers. He is the one that comforts me, consoles me and encourages me. When I finally get back to my center, things seem to become clearer, my peace returns, my confidence, and my joy.

There is a song I love: "*Jesus Is the Center of My Joy.*" I love that song because He is the center of everything in my life. I must come back to my center. He is the center that holds the reins, when I feel like I'm falling apart. I have to go to Him in prayer and allow Him to give me the next direction for my life. My life is depending on my getting back to my center. If you are feeling out of balance and your world seems to be slanted and out of focus, get to your center and let Him turn your world right side up.

Amen Sister!

"The Lord is my rock, and my fortress, and my deliverer; my God, my strength, in whom I will trust; my buckler, and the horn of my salvation, and my high tower"
(Ps. 18:2)

I Am My Wealth

I am my wealth. That sounds like a bold statement. What does that mean? I'm certainly not wealthy at this time. I don't have all the money or all the luxuries in life I would like to have, but God has given each of us gifts, talents, and abilities to produce wealth. Yes, you have it in you, the power to produce the wealth you need to live a prosperous and productive life.

So many times we are waiting for that big windfall to happen in our lives. That's why so many people play the lottery. They play the lottery thinking, "If I can hit that big jackpot, I just might get wealthy." So, they keep trying to come up with that lucky combination of numbers that will give them that expected wealth. Well, for the most part, that never happens. They may get a hit and make some money, but for most that big windfall is a one in a million chances.

God has a purpose for each of our lives. The Bible says that God has given us the ability to produce wealth (Deut 8:18). You are your own wealth. Each of us has a purpose that God has given us to produce whatever we need to live here on this earth. You have something, if you really think about it, that can produce a product, a service, an invention or idea that can produce an income for you.

We just have to look deep within ourselves and see what is it that I have that can bring me wealth. It may or may not be a million-dollar idea or invention, but it certainly can bring an added income. God never intended for us to live on one stream of income. There are times in our lives when one stream or brook will dry up; one job may go out of business; that idea is replaced or not needed any longer. But, there are always new ideas to be birthed.

What is the current trend? What does society have need of now? What about that book that will answer questions that someone might have a need for? What product will produce time management for some large corporation? What about that pie, that cake, that latest recipe or food product I can improve on that has already been manufactured?

We have the potential and the ability to be our own wealth. It's in us. If it is to be it is up to me. There is no one on earth that is more special than you are. You can do or be what you desire to be. You are God's prized possession that He uses to show forth His glory in the earth.

You can do it. Yes, you can. Fear? Do it scared. You must realize fear is an element that can be controlled. You just have to have the will and the desire to control it. Once you do the thing that you fear, it no longer has a grip on you or your future. Look fear in the face laugh and say, "You thought you had me. You thought that I wasn't going to do the very thing God intended for my life to produce the wealth He has for me. You have become my friend and not my enemy. I no longer fear you. I embrace you."

Amen Sister!

"But remember the Lord your God, for it is he who gives you the ability to produce wealth, and so confirms His covenant, which He swore to your ancestors, as it is today"
(Deuteronomy 8:18 NIV)

Don't Desert Your Desert Place

I know you think this title is a mistake and I am being redundant, really I am not. I am describing a person that would like to escape, leave, or abandon a place of barrenness, a dry season or circumstance in their life. No one likes those times when trouble comes and it seems like we are all alone and no one seemingly cares. This is a lonely time and it seems like there is no light at the end of the tunnel. This is a time when you feel lost and can't seem to get your bearings.

A desert is a place that is devoid of moisture. It's sandy, hot and nothing seems to grow. There is no vegetation or life activity. You feel like you must escape this place because, if you don't, you feel like you are going to die.

There are many examples in Scripture of those that had to pass through the desert. Moses ran away from Egypt to the desert because he had killed an Egyptian and spent 40 years on the backside of the desert. King David spent many years on the run from King Saul who was trying to kill him. Joseph was left for dead after his brothers stripped him and threw him into a pit and was traded to Pharaoh in Egypt. Jesus was led by the Holy Spirit to spend 40 days and nights in the wilderness.

It is in the desert or wilderness times when God can talk to us without interruptions and distractions. This is a time God finally has us all to Himself to love on us and to give us instructions. Most times we try to avoid those times because we don't want to be alone.

This is a time when we cry and complain to God because we are hurting or these are dry and boring times. But, God has set us aside to give us our next set of instructions. It's like God has called us in from the cares of the world and is saying to us, "Come along my child, I want to talk to you. I miss my time with you." God loves us so much and He wants the very best for us.

I've had my desert times and, yes, I know exactly how you feel. These times were probably the lowest and the loneliest times of my life, but if I had to do it all over again I would. Why would anyone want to go through those miserable lonely times and want to go back?

For me, it was during this time that I detoxed from the co-dependency, toxins, and poisons of life. My life was toxic at that time. I was broke and broken, looking for someone to fix me. Fix me! Fix me! I thought another person could fix me. Another drink could fix me. Another joint could fix me. Another night of having sex could fix me. If I could get the right job and make more money surely that would fix me. But, nothing seemed to fix me! I was broken without a remedy. So I thought.

Like most women, I lost my identity trying to be something to someone who didn't know who they were. I was looking externally instead internally. No amount of sex, drugs or money could help me. I had to get back to me and to the one that created me. I had to stop, look and listen. Most of the time God doesn't shout. He speaks in a still small quiet voice. As I began to get still, I began to hear the voice of the Holy Spirit speaking to me. I began to look forward to speaking with Him. I began to journal a lot during those intimate times so I could record my thoughts and record what He was saying to me.

I believe my journaling saved my life during those times. I prayed a lot and the floor became my best friend. It was like the floor was calling me. I had to pray to keep my sanity. My daily routine became prayer, journaling and reading the Word. That is what I did for months at a time and it brought me through that desert lonely place. It will bring you through, too.

Don't avoid your dry, arid, desert place. Let God work on you. It's a time of cutting away of all the dead things in your life so you can heal and can move into that new place He has for you. Stop kicking, screaming and complaining. Remember, you are passing through the desert and on the other side of the desert is the promised land. You can go from the desert to the promised land in one day. Don't abort your promise and don't desert your desert place.

Amen Sister!

"For the Lord, thy God hath blessed thee in all the works of thy hand: he knoweth thy walking through this great wilderness: these forty years the Lord thy God hath been with thee; thou hast lacked nothing"
(Deuteronomy 2:7)

Journal Notes

"And he went a little farther, and fell on his face, and prayed, saying, O my Father, if it be possible, let this cup pass from me: nevertheless not as I will, but as thou wilt."
Matthew 26:39

Favoring The King

When you belong to a family, many times people will say you favor your mother, father or some other member of your biological family. You have some resemblance to your mother, father, auntie, uncle or cousin, as a sign, you belong to that particular family. Sometimes the resemblance is not a physical feature. Maybe you may sound like that person, or have the same mannerisms as that person. But there is something that one can see that confirms a relationship is there.

Many times people would call my house and my daughter would answer the phone and people would think they were talking to me. My daughter and I sounded so much alike she could really pass off as her mother, but she knew better!

I was a young teen and came to visit Detroit prior to moving here. I was dating a guy and he took me to meet some of his family and friends. One lady whom I never met, when she heard I was from Pittsburgh, called my oldest sister by name and asked if we were related. She said we had to be related because I look too much like her not to be.

This resemblance is exactly what God wants us to have in the Body of Christ. He wants us to favor Him. Many times we are so busy seeking God's favor that we don't favor or resemble Him. God will give us more favor when we look like, act like, talk like and favor Him.

Before Queen Esther became the Queen, she got the favor of the eunuch that kept the women and ultimately got her a night with the King. After becoming his wife, she found favor with God to help her deliver a nation of people. Esther had the favor of God because she favored or resembled the God she served.

Do you look like your heavenly Daddy? Do you act like your Daddy? He is your Father and wants the very best and has the very best for you. Begin to change who you resemble and act like that person so others can see which family you are related to and, by your actions, they can say you look like and favor your Daddy the King of Kings.

Amen Sister!

"For we are his workmanship, created in Christ Jesus to do good works"
(Ephesian 2:10)

The Story of The Butterfly

A man found a cocoon of a butterfly. One day, a small opening appeared. He sat and watched the butterfly for several hours as it struggled to squeeze its body through the tiny hole; then it stopped as if it couldn't go further.

So the man decided to help the butterfly. He took a pair of scissors and snipped off the remaining bits of cocoon. The butterfly emerged easily but it had a swollen body and shriveled wings. The man continued to watch it, expecting that any minute the wings would enlarge and expand enough to support the body. Neither happened!

In fact, the butterfly spent the rest of its life crawling around. It was never able to fly. What the man in his kindness and haste did not understand: the restricting cocoon and the struggle required by the butterfly to get through the opening was a way of forcing the fluid from the body into the wings so that it would be ready for flight once that was achieved. Sometimes struggles are exactly what we need in our lives. Going through life with no obstacles would cripple us, we will not be as strong as we could be and we would never fly.

~Author Unknown~

no copyright infringement intended

Blind Spots

As I was driving my car one day, I was making a left turn at the intersection at the end of my street. A car was fast approaching, but I did not see it until I was in the intersection. Luckily, she could see me so I could safely complete my turn.

Continuing my drive, I thought about the "blind spots" of life. How many times have we been on a certain course of our lives and we cannot see what is up ahead of us because we have blind spots?

Or better yet, we don't want to see what's ahead because whatever it is has created a blind spot and we really can't see clearly or focus on that which is beyond our control. We need "spiritual acuity." What is acuity? Acuity is keenness of thought, vision, or hearing. We need to have a clear sharp picture of who and what we are.

What am I supposed to be doing with my life? What is my purpose? How can I find my purpose and find true fulfillment in my life? I know there is something that is missing and I have not quite found that place I'm yearning for. I know there is something else I'm supposed to be doing. What is it? I seem to be blinded from seeing clearly.

We must keep pressing for the answer until we can see clearly without any restrictions and without any blinders. You've heard the song lyrics, *"I can see clearly now that the rain is gone. It's going to be a bright sunshiny day. Now that all of the obstacles are out of my way."*

A blind spot is an obstacle that must be removed for you to have spiritual and natural acuity. It's like having cataracts on your eyes; you can see but you can't see clearly. Having a blind spot is like looking through a dirty lens or dirty windows making it hard for you to see and focus clearly.

You have to ask God to help clear up the blind spots so you can clearly see the all the plans and purposes He has for you and your life. "A blind man, Bartimaeus, was sitting by the roadside begging. When he heard Jesus of Nazareth was nearby He began to shout, "Jesus, Son of David, have mercy on me!"

Amen Sister!

"What do you want me to do for you?" Jesus asked him." The blind man said, "Rabbi, I want to see. Go, said Jesus your faith has healed you." Immediately he received his sight and followed Jesus along the road"
(Mark 10:46, 51-52)

Roadside Assistance

Every automobile owner knows there will be times when you'll have a need for roadside assistance. And, if you drive your car long enough, your tires are going to go flat and need to be changed. Your brakes are going to wear out. Oil has to be changed and maintenance is going to be needed.

As I was driving on the freeway one morning, doing about 60 miles an hour, I had a major blowout. My tire blew out so forcefully it almost blew the side panel off my car. I happened to be on my way to drop my grandchildren off at school. I started to panic but I was able to pull off safely to the side of the road.

I sat there for a few months to collect myself and, as I was sitting there, I noticed in the rearview mirror this white van pull up behind me. This was a highway assistance patrol that cruises the highways spotting cars that are broken down and in need of minor repairs, such as a tire change, dead batteries or someone may have run out of gas.

This highway assistant asked, "Ma'am, how may I assist you?" I was pleasantly surprised and I said, "Sir, I am in need of a tire change so I can continue on taking my grandchildren to school. Can you help me?" He looked at my tire and said, "You have a pretty bad blowout, but I can take care of you." So, he proceeded to change my tire as the children and I sat in the warmth of the car. This was in the winter season and in Michigan it can get pretty cold.

He finished changing the tire and put the tire that was blown in the trunk. Before he left I asked what I owed, as I had noticed others being assisted and service being compensated by their personal insurance company. He said to me, "Nothing. We are out here to assist any driver. We have cameras along the freeway and we are radioed and alerted when assistance is needed." Wow! I thanked him and was so very grateful for his assistance.

We all will need someone to assist us in our time of stress or during our time of breakdowns. There are some things in life that will cause us to have to pull over and recalculate, recalibrate, or refuel. You may need to change direction or change friends. You are going to need some roadside assistance. Do you need some gas? Do you need some air? Do you need an oil change? Do you need some brakes? You know you are on a collision course and you need to stop before you wreck yourself. You need some roadside assistance and you need it quick.

So, if you are feeling lonely and like you have been left broke down on the side of the road, ask God to come and give you some roadside assistance. He is a Friend that will stick closer than a brother. He wants to assist you and get you back on the road and pathway of life. Let Him make the minor, and sometimes major, adjustments and changes that will renew your mind and renew your faith. God is in the business of repair. He is in the business of giving you the hope and faith you need so you can go the distance and reach the desired destination point He has for you. He has an expected end for you and He is willing to aid and to help you if you let Him in. He's ready to be your roadside assistance.

Amen Sister!

"But a certain Samaritan, as he journeyed, came where he was: and when he saw him, he had compassion on him, And went to him, and bound up his wounds, pouring in oil and wine, and set him on his own beast, and brought him to an inn, and took care of him" (Luke 10:33-34)

Journal Notes

"God is our refuge and strength, a very present help in trouble." (Psalm 46:1)

The Necessity to Achieve Your Destiny

One of the most important things a person can do in life is to find their God-given purpose. Discovering your purpose will help you to know what you are destined to do on this earth. God has a purpose and a destiny for each of us. As I looked up the word destiny, it means, "bound for an appointed place; assigned to go to a place designated." You have an assignment and a specific role here on the Earth and only you can fill that which you were assigned to do. It is your appointed place that was appointed to you long before you were born. It is a place and a role that if you reach it will bring you much fulfillment in life. It's your designated place.

Another definition I found most interesting regarding destiny is that it is an "inevitable necessity." It is necessary for you to achieve and complete your destiny. God says, "For I know the plans that I have for you, declares the LORD, plans to prosper you and not to harm you, plans to give you a hope and a future" (Jeremiah 29:11).

God has great plans for your life and His plans are good and not evil. God does not want you to just achieve your destiny, but He wants you to prosper in your destiny. He wants you to achieve greatness in discovering and completing that which He has appointed you to do. No one can do what He has called you to do and no one can do it like He has called you to do it. It is important that you find your purpose in life. God created us for a purpose and on purpose.

God is a great God and inside each of us is His DNA, composition, and make-up. You were born for greatness. It's time to stretch forth your tents and enlarge your boundaries, expand and excel in the greatness of your appointed assignment.

Life is not meant to be mundane and full of blah moments. Life is meant to be exciting, going from one discovery to another. Jesus told us to have childlike faith. That means you are always on a course of wonderment, never fully being satisfied with the status quo, always on a quest for the bigness of God for your life. You don't want to ever get stagnant in desiring to achieve your destiny of greatness because it's necessary that you get to that God-expected end.

When you are destined for greatness, that means you are moving forward and you have a plan in place to get you to your goal. Yes, there may be times when you are not on your timetable, but be of good courage and continue to press on towards your mark. Authentic greatness is not a one-shot deal. It takes the time to develop but, if you stay the course, you will achieve your goal.

Just think of one important person you may know that achieved greatness. What if Martin Luther King, Jr. had not achieved his destined greatness? It would be an important piece of our history left out. Where would the Civil Rights Movement be today if he had not dreamed a dream? We are living in that dream today because it was necessary for him to achieve his greatness.

There are others in our history that achieved their destined greatness. You may not be in the historical archives of this country or a social martyr, but you too are destined to achieve your greatness - no matter how big or small you think it to be. It's your destiny. It's what God has for you. If you pursue it, and if you complete what you have been assigned to do, then you have achieved your destined greatness.

It is necessary for you to achieve your greatness. Encourage someone that is watching you achieve their greatness. We have been encouraged by the men and women that have gone on before us that made great accomplishment and achievements in their lives. It gave us hope to know that all things are possible if we only believe; if you will only believe that you have greatness inside of you.

Walking by faith and not by sight is not easy because we are so accustomed to seeing things first in the natural. God wants us to begin to develop the eyes of faith where we can see a thing before it becomes visible. God is a God of the visible and the invisible. He wants to bring those things He has for you that are invisible to the natural eye into the visible, but you have to put your faith and trust in Him.

Start by charting out your plans and how you want to accomplish them, and shortly you will begin to experience the greatness that you've always been destined to achieve. You are vital and the part you play is necessary because the world is waiting for you and counting on you to achieve your pre-destined, pre-determined role of greatness.

Amen Sister!

"These people I have formed for myself; they shall show forth my praise"
(Isaiah 43:21)

Hurt but Not Hurting

Sometimes there are circumstances in our lives that can be unavoidable that may cause us disappointing setbacks. We can manage to get through them sometimes without leaving scars. Then there are times when we may get some bumps and bruises. Yet, we continue on without truly healing, but we are hurting internally in silence.

Hurts can come from many different sources: family members, social relationships, children, employers, etc. It is inevitable. If you live on this earth long enough, you will have something or someone to hurt or betray you. How we respond to the hurt determines how we choose to get through the pain and on to our healing. Sometimes the wounds can be so deep that they require us to seek outside professional help.

If and when you decide you need help, you must be honest with yourself and with the people that are there to help you. There can be safety, comfort, and deliverance in the multitude of counselors. We must surround ourselves with people that we know have our best interest at heart and desire to help us.

Sometimes our hurts come out of the fact that we are not whole. Once you admit you are hurting, the sooner you can heal and get back on the road to wholeness. We have been wounded and it has left us fractured and divided. Just like any wound that stays open and untreated, it may set up toxins and poisons in our bodies and our emotions.

You may have been hurt but you don't have to continue hurting. Hurting means there is an ongoing level of pain in your life on a continual basis. We've all been hurt, but God does not want you to hurt continually.

There is a point when you have to decide that you want to be free from hurt and pain and have a desire to live a rich and fulfilled life.

You may have been damaged by your circumstances, but now you must get deliverance and allow the love of God, family, and friends to heal those places where you have been hurt so you can stop hurting. When you do this, you will find a place of peace and joy that you have not known. It is a real attainable place that God desires for you more than you desire for yourself. Why? Because He loves you.

This is the time my sisters to acknowledge the hurt, to stop the hurting process and becoming free, healed and whole.

Amen Sister!

"The Lord is nigh unto them that are of a broken heart; and saveth such as be of a contrite spirit"
(Ps. 34:18)

Enhanced Beauty

Everyone woman desires to have some form of beauty. This is just natural for women. We come in all shapes, sizes, and colors that set us apart from one another. Our beauty may be different from the next woman and what makes me beautiful could be different from what makes you beautiful. I believe every woman, whether she can see her beauty or not, has something about her that is beautiful. It may be her personality, her hair, her teeth, her skin, her color, etc. There is something about you that is beautiful and makes you distinctively different from other women.

There are some women that know how to take color and put outfits together that just make their outfits stand out from other women when they dress and look so beautiful. See, beauty is where you find it and it comes from within. It can be an attitude about how you feel about yourself and how you carry yourself that radiates when you are with others and they can feel your warmth. I don't believe that anyone is ugly. God made us all beautiful because we are His creation.

There is something that can enhance even the ugliest acting personality and that is the love of God that will radiate from the inside out. God can enhance the beauty and the personality of a person if they will allow that beauty to shine from the inside. You can't help but be attractive when you genuinely love God and love His people. It's like a magnet that will draw others to you and they don't know why they are drawn to you. They just know there is something different about you.

It's God's love that is shed abroad in our hearts helping us to love the most difficult person. They know that they are unloving, unkind and difficult to get along with but yet you keep on loving them. Your enhanced beauty has been enhanced by the love of God and will break down the most hateful person.

It will turn those that are against you to be for you; turn a liar and a character assassinator into a person who will come and ask your forgiveness because God has enhanced your beauty.

It can be difficult to walk with your enhanced beauty. It takes a willingness to submit to love, understanding and forgiveness and not all the ugliness of our stony hearts. I pray that when the opportunity arises the next time you will choose to walk in your enhanced beauty that comes from above.

Amen Sister!

"Whose adorning let it not be that outward adorning of plaiting the hair, and of wearing of gold, or of putting on of apparel; But let it be the hidden man of the heart, in that which is not corruptible, even the ornament of a meek and quiet spirit, which is in the sight of God of great price"
(I Peter 3:3-4)

I Am My Own Rescue

Many times we look to people, places or things to rescue us from our places of trouble, lack, pain or sorrow, but we have to realize that no one can be your rescuer. You are the only person that can rescue you from that place of rescue.

We all have those places in our lives that have held us up and have caused us to stop or stumble. Sometimes we have stayed in those places far too long and we are waiting for someone or something to come along and rescue us. No one can rescue you from any of those circumstances. You must be your own emergency rescue team. You have to make up your mind that you are tired of being stuck and want to move forward.

You have to begin to plan your escape route. "How will I get out of this mess or this place that I am in? What are some of the things I need to do to get me to this next place in my journey? What kind of help do I need from someone that has some information or answers to help me rescue myself?"

It is okay not to be okay. There is no shame in needing help. We all need someone to help or challenge us to do better, go higher and raise our expectations. What are your expectations? What do you want for yourself? What is your vision? What do you see?

To begin your rescue, you must begin to answer those questions. You have to begin to see yourself in that place of restoration. The rescue, if you are not afraid, will lead to your restoration. But, you have to want to be rescued first and then restoration will come.

The place of restoration will be that place of joy, peace, and contentment you have never known. You will begin to breathe again. You will begin to dream again. You will go from the caterpillar to the butterfly stage and come to know who you really are.

But, you have to want to dial that 911 number and say, "I have an emergency." You have to have an urgent desire on the inside of you and say I need some help because you truly are your own rescuer.

Amen Sister!

"Yea, though I walk through the valley of the shadow of death, I will fear no evil: for thou art with me; thy rod and thy staff they comfort me"
(Ps. 23:4)

Journal Notes

"I tell you the truth, my Father will give you whatever you ask in my name" (John 14:13).

New Face, Old Building

As I ride down the streets of my city, I see many older buildings now have new faces and one can almost forget what the old building looked like. The new faces on the old buildings give the buildings a new and fresh look. Some of those old buildings have been around for years and have been sold and changed owners many times over.

I can see how a new face of a building can make it appear as though that particular business is new to the neighborhood, or it's operating under a new ownership. The owners of the buildings have gone to great lengths to appear to be something new until you step inside and the inside is nothing like it appears on the outside. Now, sometimes the establishment has gone as far as to do a facelift both on the outside and the inside to really give their businesses a total makeover.

A total makeover is what God wants for each of His children. He does not want you to have just a new face and your heart or your building on the inside is not new or transformed. A new face is not authentic. It's just changing the outside but your ways, your thinking or desires are still the same. You look good to others because you can put on makeup and look as though you are happy. But, behind that face, you are broken and not whole. A little lipstick, a little makeup, and some eyeliner make you look wonderful to the outside world but you know on the inside you are sad, fearful and broken. I know because I have been there, done that, and got the tee-shirt, hat, and cup to prove it!

You have to admit to yourself when you know you are in need of repair and you are tired of faking it until you make it. A new face is not what you need. You need a total makeover. You need to let go of some things and let some new things enter in. You must begin to say to yourself, "I am sick and tired of being sick and tired."

When you decide to take that step to your total makeover and allow yourself to become healed and whole on the inside, you will never be the same. You will have the peace and joy that has escaped you for a long time. You will begin to breathe again and dream again. You will begin to laugh and enjoy life again. You will begin to enjoy being around people once again because you have allowed yourself to open up and let others into your space. You are no longer a new face and an old building. The old building just got a total makeover inside and out.

Amen Sister!

"And be not conformed to this world: but be ye transformed by the renewing of your mind, that ye may prove what is that good, and acceptable, and perfect, will of God"
(Romans 12:2)

No Longer in Bankruptcy

There are times in our lives where circumstances may happen when you are forced to make financial decisions that you agonize having to make. I have been there.

In November 2009, I lost my job due to the economic downturn. I was a 15-year veteran sales rep that sold cars in one of the largest and most profitable dealerships in Metro Detroit, Michigan. Many dealerships were closing, plants were downsizing, retiring and laying off employees and car sales were at an all-time low. As salespeople, we were struggling to meet quotas and barely making enough money to pay our bills. Our 401K's became 101K's and the overall economic climate was very gloomy. We all went to work each day not knowing if it would be our last day and for some of us, it was.

I remember that day. I continued to show up, no matter what, because I liked what I did and because I needed the paycheck. Let's be honest. We go to work mostly because it is a means to an end to pay our bills. We don't go to work just because we want something to do. We go because we need a way to support our lifestyles whatever that may be.

As I said, I remember going to work that day and decisions had been made by the management who would be let go. I was one of those that would be let go. Now, you have to understand the car business is a highly revolving door kind of industry. Everyone cannot endure the long hours and work in the uncertainty of commission pay. I happened to have loved it and during the "glory days," it paid well.

Although I loved my job, I had mixed emotions. I was really growing weary of the day-to-day routine and I knew it was time for something different. I must say I was not surprised and I was relieved when I was told it was my last day.

God had prepared me at least **some** years before that this day was coming, I just did not really want to let go because of some of the perks that went along with the job, like driving a new car free of charge.

I was struggling, as well as the majority of the sales personnel, to make house payments and make ends meet. The day came that I had to face the fact I could no longer make those payments. After trying to work with my mortgage company to no avail, foreclosure and bankruptcy were my only option.

Today, I am proud to say God has allowed me to reclaim my home. I have made arrangements with the loan guarantors, paying back a fraction of what I would have to pay if I had continued with my original mortgage. In less than six months from the writing of this book, my house will be paid for. I lost 15 years off the original 30-year mortgage, and $70,000 in debt wiped out. I now pay less than half the monthly payment, with zero percent interest, because it is an agreement and not a loan! Wow! What can I say except, God is good!

So, my Sisters, I want to encourage you. What God did for me He can and will do for you. God's bank is not empty! No matter what has happened in your life, going forward, make an honest assessment, eliminating and liquidating those things that cause you clutter and pain. If you do this you, too, will no longer be in bankruptcy.

Make an investment, make a deposit, and watch how much fuller and richer your life will be.

Amen Sister!

"And we know that all things work together for good to them that love God, to them who are the called according to his purpose" "What shall we then say to these things? If God be for us, who can be against us? (Romans 8:28, 31)

Intercessory Prayer

Jesus, our High Priest is also our Great Intercessor. He is the One that goes to the Father on our behalf. He left us a model of intercessory prayer in John 17:1-26. An intercessor prays, petitions in favor of another, or stands in the gap between the person and the Father in prayer.

I consider this a privilege that God has given me to write *Amen Sister!* It is a tool used to touch God on behalf of women. This, my sister, is a high honor. This is my prayer:

My prayer for you, my sister of every race, creed, and color, no matter what your position is in life is, that above all things that you may prosper. I pray that you become whole in your body, soul, and spirit; that you will dream big and see those dreams become a reality.

I pray that God will comfort you when you're lonely, hurt, rejected or misunderstood; especially when you know that you've done your very best. I pray that when you make a mistake and fall down you will find the strength to get back up and try, try, and keep on trying. Never stop trying. Always have a loving and forgiving heart; never allowing bitterness to take root.

I pray that you learn to love yourself, nurture yourself and accept yourself as God loves and accepts you. You, my sisters, are accepted in the Beloved. Nothing can separate you from the love of God. You are wonderfully and fearfully made. You have been designed by the hand of the Almighty God. None is like you, not in all the earth.

I pray that you will use all your gifts and talents for God to the best of your ability and that you would reach back to the next generation and sow your life into them. I pray you love your fellow sisters and be willing and ready to help when needed, as none of your gifts are too large or too small; they are necessary and they are needed.

I pray you won't leave the earth until you have completed all those things that God has given you to do. I pray the vision He has placed inside of you will come full term and that you will birth and not abort. You are pregnant with possibility and potential. You're God's Woman.

Amen Sister!

I pray that your daily portion would be, "And the peace of God, which passeth all understanding, shall keep your hearts and minds through Christ Jesus" (Phil 4:7)

Bringing Closure

The bringing of closure is so important to begin to move in a new and fresh direction. In my own life, I've had to bring closure many times and in many ways. I've had to bring closure in marriage resulting in divorce, relationships, losing a job, losing my home, the death of my parents and death of some friends, and much more. But, I found myself much stronger after I decided to finally bring closure.

Sometimes bringing closure is difficult to do because we like to hold on to what is familiar to us and often times it can be downright scary. I have to admit there were some times while moving in the direction God would have me go, I hesitated because it was a little frightening. That new place seemed so big and so vast and I felt so inadequate and unprepared. But closure was necessary to get me to that new place.

These journal writings are a result of my bringing closure to a relationship. I was in a relationship with a man that I fell in love with. We started out as friends and it evolved into a relationship that lasted roughly four years. I said to him one day, "I am not a girlfriend. I am a wife. I am no longer going to continue to date you. You have to make a decision how important this relationship is to you and whether it is important enough to keep."

He told me he knew I was his wife but he never moved any further in his decision. So, after a few months, we stopped seeing each other. I had to bring closure. I had to heal and move on. Was it easy? No, it was not. It was very painful but the process had to take place. Am I glad I made that decision? Yes, I am. You see I was not willing to compromise my standards. We were never sexually intimate and I knew that if I continued this relationship something would happen to change that, and for my own good it was best we end our relationship.

The good of all this, my Sisters, is that I am able to share my life and my testimonies that I can relate to you. I can relate if you are having a difficult time bringing closure to a particular area of your life. Be encouraged to know you can do it. You must do it so you can have all that God has for you. You have new doors and new opportunities that are waiting for you to explore. You have new people you have to meet and they have to meet you. You have a destiny, a hope, and a future.

I knew when the Holy Spirit gave me the word "closure" it was the end of this journal and it is time to move on to my next project. I am bringing closure to "Amen Sister!" on a positive note, knowing there were things in my own life that I had to evaluate and bring closure to.

It is closure, for now, my Sisters, but rest assured it is not the end. I am praying for my Sisters of every race, creed, and culture.

I love you.

We are better together.

Amen Sister!

CPSIA information can be obtained
at www.ICGtesting.com
Printed in the USA
FSHW010923190519
58262FS